Onions

Onions

A CELEBRATION OF THE ONION

THROUGH

RECIPES, LORE, AND HISTORY

Mara Reid Rogers

ILLUSTRATIONS BY JACK LUTZOW

ADDISON-WESLEY PUBLISHING COMPANY

Reading, Massachusetts Menlo Park, California New York
Don Mills, Ontario Wokingham, England Amsterdam Bonn
Sydney Singapore Tokyo Madrid San Juan
Paris Seoul Milan Mexico City Taipei

The following recipes are reprinted with permission:

"Irma Rhode's Onion Sandwiches" from *The James Beard Celebration Cookbook* by the James Beard Foundation, edited by Barbara Kafka. Text copyright © 1990 by the James Beard Foundation.

"Papaya and Shrimp Salad" from *The Original Thai Cookbook* by Jennifer Brennan. Published by Perigree Books, copyright © 1981 by Jennifer Brennan.

"Garlic Rosemary Jelly" from *Gourmet* magazine. Copyright © 1994 by The Condé Nast Publications Inc.

Library of Congress Cataloging-in-Publication Data

Rogers, Mara Reid.
   Onions : a celebration of the onion through recipes, lore, and history / Mara Reid Rogers.
      p.   cm.
   Includes bibliographical references and index.
   ISBN 0-201-62680-2
   1. Cookery (Onions). 2. Onions I. Title.
TX803.05R64 1995
641.6′525—dc20   95-14034
                                          CIP

Jacket design by Jean Seal
Jacket and text illustrations by Jack Lutzow
Text design by Jennie Bush, Designworks
Set in 10-point Galliard by Carol Woolverton Studio

1 2 3 4 5 6 7 8 9-DOH-9998979695
First printing, May 1995

To my husband, Mark Hill,

to whom I am dedicated—

for his enthusiasm, generosity, and caring

Onions

Come, follow me by the smell,

Here are delicate onions to sell;

I promise to use you well.

They make the blood warmer,

You'll feed like a farmer;

For this is every cook's opinion,

No savoury dish without an onion;

But, lest your kissing should be spoiled,

Your onions must be thoroughly boiled:

Or else you may spare

Your mistress a share,

The secret will never be known:

She cannot discover

The breath of her lover,

But think it as sweet as her own.

—Jonathan Swift, *Verses for Fruitwomen*

Contents

PART ONE

PART TWO   *Recipes*

Acknowledgments

Thank you to Elizabeth Carduff who saw me for the onion enthusiast that I am; my agent Angela Miller for her help; Judith Clarke Lydic and Shelia Petree for their valuable aid in recipe testing, creative solutions, and discerning tastebuds; Chef Morris of The Art Institute of Atlanta for his interest in the project and helping me find Judith and Shelia; Wayne Mininger of the National Onion Association for his insights into the world of onions; Nancy Teksten of the National Onion Association for her inestimable contributions; Francesca Trubia for her knowledge of Italian cooking; Linda Dickert of Specialty Brands Incorporated for information on Fleischmann's yeast and for "talking bread" with me; Jan Longone for her invaluable advice and support; Judith H. Ho of the National Agricultural Library special collections department for her research; the Atlanta-Fulton library reference department; Ron L. Engeland for his vast understanding of garlic; Susan Carol Aker for her restaurant knowledge; Jack Lutzow for his illustrations; Laura Lensgraf for her suggestions; Evie Righter for her editing; Kim Hertein for her expertise; and Susan Lohafer for her talent.

I would also like to thank the following people and commissions for sharing their knowledge of onions: Paula Fouchek of the Texas Fresh Promotional Board; Robin Raiford of the Vidalia Onion Committee; Barbara A. Rogers of the Vegetable Improvement Center; Kathleen McCelland, publisher of *The Historical Gardener* newsletter; Larry Arbini of Arbini Farms; Louis L. Soucie of Sixstar Promotions; the California Imperial Sweet Onion Commission; Maui's Farmers' Cooperative; Walla Walla Sweet Onion Commission; Joel Patraker of Greenmarket Farmers' Market; Raymond

Sokolov; The Produce Marketing Association Information Center; Elizabeth Schneider; Jeni Northrop of the United Fruit and Vegetable Association; Mike Thornton of the University of Idaho College of Agriculture; Lynn Jensen of Oregon State University; Jim Vaux of Asgrow Seed Company; Nick Molenaar of Crookham Company; Jim Robison of Robison Ranch; and Beth Benjamin of Shepherd's Garden Seeds Company.

The Inspiring Onion

*The onion and its satin wrappings is among the
most beautiful of vegetables, and is the only one
that represents the essence of things. It can almost
be said to have a soul.*

—Charles Dudley Warner, *My Summer in a Garden* (1870)

ON THE TRAIL OF THE ONION

This book is an exploration into the world of onions—succulent, heavy bulbs; willowy scallions; sturdy, muscular leeks; sophisticated shallots; delicate chives; and full-throated, lusty garlic. When I say "onion," I mean all of these edible plants, with flavors ranging from creamy sweet to biting hot. My focus is not on the exotica, but on the extraordinary qualities of the ordinary onion and its relatives.

To tell you about onions, I've drawn from history and lore, science and literature. Did you know that bulb onions and garlic were part of the Egyptian mummification process and have been found in tombs? and that throughout American history, cowboys called onions "skunk eggs"? The Bible mentions not only onions, but garlic and leeks as well. The medicinal uses of this plant are not just ancient superstition: Today, research shows that the bulb onion may help prevent the common cold, while the sulphur-bearing oils in onions and garlic may thwart cancer in its initial stages.

Like most people, I used to take the onion for granted. However, in working on this book, I began a journey of discovery that took me far into the past and all around the world. It began with memories of being a barefoot child and feeling the earth between my toes. I used to pull up the first onions in our lush garden. I tugged and tugged on the strong, tubular shoots, as the bruised green leaves emitted their fragrance of protest until finally I won the tug-of-war. Heavy, soil-laden, shiny white bulbs would slip from the ground as the earth let go, and I would tumble over backwards. My dug-up treasure was destined for my mother's wicker gardening basket, then into the skillet for the evening meal.

After dinner, my mother would read stories to me, like *Alice's Adventures in Wonderland*. The tale I remember best was the terrifying story of the Seven-of-Spades, who brought the Queen-of-Heart's cook "tulip roots instead of onions." For this mistake he was beheaded. Now that I'm older and appreciate onions, I can sympathize with the Queen and her wrath—but beheading? That still seems a little severe. . . .

As a teenager some years later in drawing class, I discovered the beauty of the shape of the onion itself. With true, natural elegance, it impressed me as one of nature's masterpieces. Its seven shiny, papery, semi-translucent wrappings—sometimes red, purple, white, or gold—were pristine, satiny veils, a cloak for the spiral rounds of perfectly formed flesh. As Robert Louis Stevenson said, the onion is "the rose of roots."

The essence of the onion is captured, too, in simplified botanical terms. The common onion, known as *Allium cepa*—in Latin *Allium* means garlic; *cepa* onion—is the edible bulb of a plant belonging to the botanical genus *Alliaceae* (or onion family). The word "allium," however, has been adapted as the generic name for every member of the *Alliaceae* group, which also includes garlic, the leek, chive, scallion, and shallot. These, with the bulb onion, are herbs that can be used not only as aromatics but as vegetables. There are some five hundred species of the *Alliaceae* in the northern hemisphere. Many of them are edible, but not necessarily good to eat; some are grown solely for their beautiful flowers, and many still grow wild in the prairies, fields, and mountains. *Alliaceae* is part of an even larger botanical family—*Liliaceae*—or lily family. Easter lilies and onions! In the pure light of science, they meet as relatives.

For me, though, all the stories, drawings, and dictionary definitions on onions are far too abstract. To really know the onion, I had to start cooking with it. This astounding vegetable came full circle in my life when I tossed it into my weathered, cast-iron skillet. I sliced it, diced it, minced it, and sautéed it (and its relatives) all the way through cooking school. I learned during those months that there is no more reliable vegetable, none so able to please, to respond positively in almost every recipe I and you may try.

After all is said and done, short of burning it, it is hard to ruin an onion. That is why budding chefs are so grateful to it. As each burner of my stove labored under the weight of yet another pot of stew or sauce, I could count on the onions in those pans to stand the heat. Unlike other vegetables that suffer when overcooked—mushy carrots or string beans gone gray—onions survive, unless burned to an absolute crisp, and, even then, I've seen some people savor them.

I was learning what the world already knew: The onion is a most important culinary ingredient. Wherever you travel and dine, you find them—from the garlic-scented mayonnaise of France (*aïoli*), to Scotland's chicken and leek soup (cockaleekie), to Thailand's condiment of crumbled fried onions. Almost every culture cooks with onions. They are the conductor of the kitchen's orchestra of ingredients, and just like an orchestra without a tempo, dishes without onions lack unity and flair. The common bulb onion is in greater demand in the kitchen than any other vegetable; in fact, today Americans every year eat 15½ pounds of onions per person, up 56 percent since 1982! When the cupboard is almost bare, the chances are you can still find an onion.

So why is it we know so little about our favorite vegetable? I decided to write this book when I realized how misunderstood the onion and its relatives are. In my gustatory journey, I aspired to unravel the mysteries about onions in general, discredit the myths, and support the truths. I wanted to share my passion and curiosity about this staple food. To do this, I had to cast a wide net. My research involved not only tasting and reading, but traveling and talking. Most of all, it involved listening to a variety of people—home cooks, botanists, historians, farmers, and seedsmen.

I began by discovering that the first onion, species uncertain, existed in prehistoric times. I also learned, not surprisingly, that today's onion-eater rarely knows how to distinguish the different categories and types of this basic food, let alone the distinctions among its many varieties. For example, there's an entire world of older onion varieties—sometimes called "heirloom" onions, known only to the home gardener, or the seedsman with a passion for "novelty" vegetables. Few know that a ramp is a variety of wild onion, with a nose-blasting scent, even when cooked. I learned this firsthand at a ramp festival near the Great Smoky Mountains of Tennessee. The much more innocuous "pearl onions," it turns out, are not the baby onions they appear to be but are a mature member of the onion family. And did you know that when you buy "Bermuda" onions at the supermarket that they are mislabeled? For about eight years now, "genuine" Bermuda onions haven't been available in the United States, and are obtainable only from the Caribbean countries, although the name lives on.

A name does make a difference. The fact that some cookbook authors are still claiming that a scallion can be substituted for a shallot is not only erroneous but outrageous!

COOKING WITH THE ONION FAMILY

The flavor and texture of an onion can turn a dish from bland and boring to flavorful and lively. Onions can render a dish down home and earthy, or elevate it to elegance and sophistication. While one member of the onion clan can be mild in both flavor and scent, another can be pungent, with eye-watering sting. Nothing awakens the tastebuds or satisfies the soul like the aroma of onions slowly simmering in a skillet, baking in a pie, or bubbling in a soup. These are the reasons why I never tire of cooking with onions, from appetizers to desserts.

Their appeal is as practical as it is tempting. They are inexpensive and plentiful throughout the year, no matter where you live. A little of the onion or one of its relatives can go a long way. Each member of the onion family has its purpose, and each has a place in a menu—from shallots in a subtle sauce to boiling onions in a hearty stew. They store well; in fact, there is an entire onion category named for its longevity—the "storage" onion. Low in calories and high in fiber, they meet today's standards for healthy food. They move easily from cold- to warm-weather dishes. Onions are easy to prepare. They can be creamed, baked, grilled, smoked, roasted, pickled, puréed, French fried, scalloped, stir-fried, sautéed, or stuffed. They are often enjoyed raw. The onion is a vegetable laureate, distinctive in flavor and matchless in versatility.

Today, the onion is a bold culinary force. It can be the deciding factor between a so-so dish and a stupendous one, the star that gives sparkle to a dish, adding flavor, color, texture, and interest. In many national dishes, the onion is vital. For example, without the crunch of a crisp slice of raw onion, the American hamburger, as many know and love it, would simply not be the same.

Onions have made their way into culinary legend, but some of the most amazing stories about them are absolutely true. One night I was awakened by the sound of ripping. Whatever could that be? I asked myself, still half-asleep, tracking the sound to the kitchen. What did I see? Sam, my big tabby cat, was standing on the kitchen table, peeling onions. Yes, peeling them! With his teeth, he was removing layer after layer. There were miniature piles of onion skins on the kitchen floor, and a few precious bulbs still untouched. Night after night, Sam continues this ritual, unless I remember to drape the onion bowl with a towel. If Sam could talk, I believe he'd tell me onions taste good and who am I to argue?

THE ONION FARES WELL

Here is a sampling of restaurants across America that proves how inventive cooking with onions can be.

- In Cambridge, Massachusetts, Anago Bistro serves *savory smoked salmon tart with leeks and salad greens*.
- Vidalia in Washington, D.C., offers *spiced onion rings* with *onion mustard*.
- Ciboulette in Atlanta, Georgia, serves *wild mushroom and asiago ravioli with roasted garlic jus* as an appetizer.
- The signature salad of the Sheraton Seattle hotel's restaurant is *sweet and bitter greens with roasted beet and shallot vinaigrette*.
- Zinfandel in Chicago has a seasonal *spring potato soup of Yukon golds, artichokes, and wild ramps*.
- The Stinking Rose, a restaurant named after the benevolent garlic bulb, is located in San Francisco, California. Its theme—garlic. The restaurant touts such dishes as *ballpark 40 clove garlic chicken sandwich* and side dishes from *garlic potato chips* to *roasted garlic bulb* to *marinated garlic olives*. They even serve *château de garlic*—you guessed it—garlic wine!

About the Recipes in This Book

In the following pages, you will learn the characteristics of each member of the onion family, how to grow these plants and what to look for when purchasing them, and, of course, how to store and use them. You will know what to do when you buy your first bunch of Chinese yellow chives, or come home with a bag of shallots or a bunch of scallions. Just as I was inspired by spring onions, a crop of baby leeks, or a bulk bag of garlic from the farmers' market, I hope you will dream up ways of using onions in soups and salads, appetizers and entrees, condiments, and even desserts.

I have included both classic and original preparations, each with my own personal touch—employing perhaps a preparation technique from another culture or an unusual ingredient combination. Adhering to the current wisdom on healthful eating, I have tried to create recipes that are sensible. If you are on a restricted diet, you can adapt the recipes, modifying them to your own requirements. I have cut down on fat, sodium, and cholesterol, but each dish is a balance of delicious taste and good nutrition. For vegetarians, there are some meatless recipes, including Sea Scallops with Braised Leeks and White Wine, and Tomato and Black Olive Onion Pizza. And for those special occasions when anything goes, I have tucked in a few rich recipes like Spring Vidalia Onion Pie.

In the pages of this cookbook, the onion reigns supreme, but it is not always the dominant flavor. Yes, you will find the familiar and scrumptious golden fried rings, but you will also find the onion as a background flavor, a texture, a binder for other ingredients, or a touch of color. In every case, though, the onion's contribution is vital. Onions, shallots, leeks, and garlic are much more than seasoning; chives and scallions are more than mere garnishes. You will discover, as I have, that this common vegetable is very far from commonplace.

ALLIUM ACCOLADES

- Ancient Egyptians thought so highly of onions that they inserted them into the wrapping of mummies and even into the deceased's eye sockets. Some Egyptologists believe that this was an attempt to rouse the dead into breathing again.
- Several vegetables were sculpted in precious metals by Egyptian artisans to be used as temple offerings to the gods by Egyptian priests; only onions were ever crafted in gold.
- Caesar's armies carried leeks to the British Isles, where they became so highly valued by the Welsh that they chose them for their national emblem and wore them in their hat bands when riding into battle.
- Antony and Cleopatra worshiped onions, believing them to be a symbol of eternity, based upon the concentric circles of their internal structure.
- The emperor Nero loved leeks and drank a potion made with leeks every day, convinced that it improved his singing voice.
- Roman gladiators were rubbed with onion juice to firm their muscles, and early Olympic athletes were advised to eat onions to help "lighten" the blood.
- In medieval Europe onions were considered so valuable that they were used as rent payment and as wedding gifts.
- Onions were prescribed to alleviate headaches, snake bites, and hair loss in the Middle Ages.
- Onion blossoms are known as puffballs because the wind sweeps them away like puffs of smoke. In Ireland there is a superstition that the leprechauns choose the farmhouse with the largest puffballs for their summer revels; and that farmer, as a reward for leaving his onions intact, is rewarded by the Little People with his chickens laying twice as many eggs for the remainder of the year.
- During the Civil War, General Ulysses S. Grant sent an urgent message to the War Department, saying, "I will not move my army without onions." The next day three cartloads were on their way to the front. The reason: General Grant, some thought, was convinced that onions prevented dysentery and other ills.

1

The Onion Takes Root

2

Understanding Onions

3

An Onion Sampler

4

Growing Onions

CHAPTER ONE

The Onion Takes Root

THE HISTORY OF THE ONION

Onions, garlic, and leeks are mentioned in the earliest human records and may be the oldest of all cultivated vegetables: People have been growing them for more than 5,000 years. The earliest onion, though, existed long before farming or even writing was invented. It didn't look like any of the varieties we know today. Probably, it resembled a reed—thin and flat, with an underdeveloped bulb, something like a cross between present-day varieties of wild onions and our supermarket scallions.

That first onion had a strong, distinctive odor, especially when bruised. Its pungent scent may well have attracted the early foragers. "The most ancient form of human economic organization was the hunter or gatherer clan," wrote Jay Pascal Anglin and William J. Hamblin in *World History to 1648*. Before 10,000 B.C., primitive hunter-gatherers routinely scavenged for wild onions, following their noses or looking for the slender green shoots marking treasure below.

The first plants to be domesticated were the ones that stood out, either because they were more edible in that they had the largest edible parts or had some other characteristic that drew attention. Waverley Root, author of *Food*, writes, "[The onion] was already being cultivated by prehistoric man when [he was] still in the collecting stage which preceded the pastoral and agricultural stages. . . . " At first, man had to travel great distances to find food, but once he learned the rudiments of agriculture, he could grow plants closer to home, in abundant quantities. Enter the onion. Onions may have been one of the earliest crops not only because they commanded interest, but because they were less perishable than other foods of the time, were transportable, were easy to grow, and could be grown in a variety of soils and climates.

Onions could survive the devastations of nature. The edible root, protected beneath the soil line, could withstand the ravages of water and sun, heat and cold. Hardy in itself, the onion was useful for sustaining human life. It prevented thirst and could be dried and preserved for later consumption, when food might be scarce. Very likely, this humble vegetable was a staple in the prehistoric diet. While hunters hunted, gatherers were searching for onions.

ONION ETYMOLOGY

According to Martin Elcort, author of *The Secret Life of Food,* "*onion* is a doublet of the word *union*—meaning both words are similar but entered the language through different routes. The word was created by adding the onion-shaped letter *o* to the word *union,* yielding the new spelling *ounion.* The letter *u* was later dropped to create the modern spelling. A union is something that is indivisible and which, if taken apart, is destroyed in the process, like an onion. The original root of the word is the Latin *un,* meaning 'the number one,' the only number that is not further divisible."

Ancient Civilizations: Sumer and Egypt

The written history of mankind and the written history of the onion may have begun roughly in the same place—the southernmost tip of Mesopotamia. The Sumerians, who probably arrived there around 3500 B.C., may well have invented writing, and with it, the earliest known civilization. Although we don't know where the onion originated, its written history seems to have begun in Sumer, and there is evidence that the Sumerians were growing onions as early as 2500 B.C.

The Sumerians used a wedge-shaped stylus to "write" syllables on clay tablets, which were then baked. This form of writing is known as cuneiform script. Archaeologists found such a tablet dating from around 2400 B.C. bearing an inscription in Sumerian recording a citizen's complaint about the misuse of public property. Apparently, a local bureaucrat (the *ishakku*) had been using animals belonging to the temple for work in his own field. In part, the inscription reads: "The oxen of the Gods plowed the *ishakku*'s onion patches. . . . "

This attention to public morality is particularly interesting, because during the first Babylonian dynasty—Babylon was the ancient capital city of Babylonia in southern Mesopotamia—the oldest known body of law was created. Developed during the reign of King Hammurabi (1792–1750 B.C.), this compilation is known as the Code of Hammurabi. It is the most complete collection of Babylonian laws and includes an early provision for public welfare: On one day of each month, needy persons were to receive about a "gallon" of bread and some onions.

In dynastic Egypt, the combination of bread, raw onions, and beer was supposedly the main diet of the peasant. Workers building the Great Pyramid at Giza (begun by King Cheops of Egypt in the 27th century B.C.) were fed a diet of mostly onions and garlic. Herodotus, the Greek "Father of History," later saw and recorded an inscription on the pyramid, no doubt written by an ancient bookkeeper. It said the laborers had consumed "onions, radishes, and garlic, costing 1,600 talents." Although the exact worth of 1,600 talents (a unit of weight and value) cannot be precisely translated into today's dollar, estimates I have read range from $200,000 to $2,000,000. Onions and garlic were clearly of value, and no small item in the construction budget for this grand monument.

Throughout world history, onions have been thought of as food for the poor, since the strong odor and taste offended the palates of the wealthy. Yet history also reveals that onions were grown in the gardens of kings, such as Ur-Nammu of Ur (a city-state in Sumer) in 2100 B.C. and Merodach-Baladan of Babylon, in 716 B.C. The prestige of the onion rose even higher in ancient Egypt, where it was almost deified.

The onion's spherical shape and concentric rings made it a powerful symbol for the universe and for the sun god. The round layers of the onion represented heaven, hell, earth, and the universe. Later, this quality of wholeness was captured in the Latin word *unio* or *uniorem,* meaning "unity," from the root *un,* meaning the number one. *Unio* also referred to a single large pearl, another product of nature formed by many concentric layers; perhaps, by analogy, *unio* which is the stem for our word "onion," was applied, in particular, to white onions. In any case, the form of the onion was a powerful image of divine perfection.

The vegetable itself was sometimes treated as a sacred object. Some Egyptians would swear their oaths on an onion, as a guarantee of good faith. Priests would not eat them, maybe as a sign of religious commitment or as a way of impressing the public with a feat of abstinence. Mourners and worshipers would sometimes bring onions as funeral gifts during the Old Kingdom period (c. 2615 to 2175 B.C.). A basket of onions was second only to bread as a valued offering. Onions appear in chapel altar pictures; in fact, Egyptian craftsmen would sculpt several vegetable forms in precious metals for the priests to use as temple offerings to the gods. However, only one vegetable was represented in gold—the "one" that stood for the universe.

Still, the most intriguing fact about the onion as it existed in Egypt is in its relationship to an afterlife. According to James E. Harris and Kent R. Weeks, authors of *X-Raying the Pharaohs:* "They [Egyptians] recognized death, of course, but for them it was not the final, absolute end. Rather, it was the continuation of life in a different form. What they enjoyed and found pleasant in this life they tried to take with them in the next. To insure this, techniques of mummification were developed."

In this process, onions and garlic had both a spiritual and a physical role to play. The body of a deceased person had to be preserved for eternity to ensure a "lasting home for the soul," and offerings, including food, were placed in or near the tomb to be on hand in the afterlife. Sometimes real food was used, but sometimes relief scenes or sculpture depicted the items, which became "real" through rites of magic. Some Egyptologists theorize that onions may have been used because their strong scent and/or magical powers would prompt the dead to breathe again. Other Egyptologists believe it was because onions and garlic were known for their strong antiseptic qualities, which were construed as magical, and would be handy in the afterlife.

Garlic was found in King Tut's tomb (died c. 1352 B.C.), and onions were discovered behind the eyelids of Rameses IV (died 1150 B.C.), perhaps to simulate eye sockets and give the desired lifelike appearance. For the same reason, it is thought that the skin of the onion was sometimes placed over the eyes of the dead. In addition, onions as well as garlic might be placed on the mummies or in their hands. In their conception of eternity, as in their model of the universe, the Egyptians showed reverence for the onion.

Early Greece and Rome

We do not know exactly when the onion reached Greece, although it may have been, at the latest, during the Early Bronze Age (c. 3000 B.C.). According to Don and Patricia Brothwell in *Food in Antiquity,* Theophrastus (born c. 372 B.C.; died c. 287 B.C.), considered the founder of botany whose works include the *Natural History of Plants* and *On the Origin of Plants* wrote of several onion and garlic varieties, noting that Cyprian—a type of garlic apparently used raw—had a special virtue: "when pounded, it makes a foaming dressing."

According to Waverley Root in *Food,* by the time of the Athenian statesman Pericles (born c. 495 B.C.; died c. 429 B.C.), the market of Athens was selling edible plants. Most of these vegetables were expensive and sold in small quantities, but onions were abundant—and affordable. That is probably why they were widely consumed, especially by the poor. It may also be why they were fed to soldiers. In *The Iliad,* an epic poem attributed to the Greek poet Homer (9th or 8th century B.C.), Hecamede serves wine to the warriors Nestor and Nachaon, and, as a relish, sets before them an onion on a bronze dish.

In Rome, too, onions were often thought of as a food for the working class, the poor, and the military. Onions were fed to warriors and their horses, as was garlic, which was pledged to Mars, the god of war. The first written reference to the onion is by Horace (65 to 8 B.C.), who included it in *Odes*, 1, 31. In the translation by Burton Raffel in *The Essential Horace*, the stanza of the poem which refers to onions reads:

> Merchants favored by the gods, permitted
> To cross the Atlantic three times a year,
> Or four, and return. No, it's olives for me,
> And onions, and mallow.

The Ancient Roman was not always a soldier; sometimes, he was an epicure, and it was probably for the aristocrat, the person of cultivated taste, that the earliest cookbook was written. Its author was the Roman gourmet Apicius, and its title was *De Re Coquinaria*— or *De Re Culinaria* (Of Culinary Matters). In *The Delectable Past*, Esther B. Aresty writes, "The only known copies of the so-called Apicius cookbook date from the eighth and ninth centuries." Apparently, this handwritten book held the interest of an audience, since "there is no doubt that it was in use until the fifteenth century . . . " Since the recipes in the Apicius book called for almost all the members of the onion family, we can deduce that these vegetables were in some favor at higher socioeconomic levels at that time in Rome.

In his recipes, Apicius excluded only chives, with *cepa* (onion), *aleum alium* (garlic), *cepula* (Welsh onion), *cepa Ascalonia* (shallot), *cepa pallachana* (spring onion), and *porrus* (leek) all called for. Almost all were incorporated as an aromatic or flavoring in small amounts—that is, as an ingredient in dressings and sauces— rather than as a vegetable, whole or raw. One example is puree of lettuce leaves with onions. The leek, however, was featured as a vegetable in several recipes, including one in which they were boiled, then served as is with a little wine and a few other flavorings.

We know onions were grown in Pompeii, the ancient city of Campania, Italy. "Pompeiian onions" were praised by the first agricultural writer of the Christian era, Columella of Spain (born 1st century A.D.). He recommended that these onions be dried, then preserved by being pickled in vinegar and brine. Excavators of the doomed city Pompeii (destroyed in A.D. 79) discovered the remains of a basket of onions in one of the city's brothels.

The Middle Ages

"The three main vegetables of the European table during the Middle Ages were beans, cabbage, and onions," writes Reay Tannahill in *Food in History*. During this period (A.D. 500 to 1500), onions were popular with the poor, but also gained favor with the well-to-do and respectable. At this time, the nobility set the standards for husbandry. Following the crowning of Charlemagne (born c. 742; died 814) as Emperor by Pope Leo III in Rome in 800 A.D., Charlemagne ordered onions to be planted in his domains. Five centuries later, according to Waverley Root in *Food*, Alexander Neckam (born 1157; died 1217), as abbot at Cirencester, Gloucestershire, gave his own boost to the status of onions, by deeming them fit for noble gardens, and, Root adds, "set the example by growing them in his own."

Old World and New

No one knows exactly where *A. cepa*—our common onion originated, but most authorities think it somehow came into existence as a result of early cultivation of a wild onion from either the southwest corner of Asia or central Asia. How it journeyed outward from there is still a mystery, since the advent of most members of the onion family predates written history. There is even some question about its central Asia roots.

Waverley Root has puzzled this deeper: "Can it be the place of origin of this vegetable is where no one has thought to look for it, in America?" In *Food*, he suggests that one way to answer this question is to identify the world's oldest onion and then backtrack to learn its actual origin. As an investigative strategy, this seems a little oversimplified. Even though there are currently hundreds of wild onion species growing almost everywhere in Europe, Asia, and North America, it is hard to pick the oldest. Many of the wild ancestors of today's varieties have become extinct, making it impossible for botanists to regrow the family tree, even in theory.

Nevertheless, some food historians suspect that onions really are indigenous to the western hemisphere, and with hundreds of wild onion members growing across the continent, it is probable that onions were cultivated simultaneously in a number of different places. After all, the "New World" wasn't exactly new. Civilizations prospered in North America long before Columbus arrived in 1492, and wild alliums were frequent. Moreover, evidence of wild garlic and ramps (a form of wild onion) has been found in shards of pre-Columbian cooking artifacts. Native American Indians used wild onions in a variety of ways, eating them raw or cooked, as a seasoning or as a vegetable. Such onions were also used in syrups, as poultices, as an ingredient in dyes, and even as toys.

There is testimony from later periods, as well. In the late 1600s, Père Marquette, a French Jesuit missionary and explorer, told of being saved from starvation by eating native wild American tree onions and nodding onions when his explorations took him from Green Bay, Wisconsin, to a point on the southern shore of Lake Michigan, where he found the ground covered with wild onions. Some think the site's modern name—Chicago—is derived from the Indian word *checagou,* which refers to the pungent smell of the plants.

Wild onions aside, we do know cultivated alliums arrived with Columbus on his second visit to the New World. In 1493, he returned to these shores with seventeen ships and twelve hundred men. As Raymond Sokolov tells us in *Why We Eat What We Eat,* those ships carried, "literally, the seeds of colonization." Besides animals, Columbus ferried seeds and cuttings across the Atlantic. According to Sokolov, he "brought what was needed to start plantations, orchards, and kitchen gardens, the wherewithal to grow onions, grapes, fruit, radishes, and sugarcane."

Probably what is now the Dominican Republic became the seeding ground for onions, and from there spread rapidly to Mexico, Central America, South America, and of course, North America, where Native American Indians were already used to the flavor of wild onions. Thereafter, onions continued to play an important role in the colonization of the New World. The Pilgrims brought the Eurasian *Allium cepa*—the bulb onion—on their transatlantic journey on the *Mayflower*. According to diaries of colonists, onions were planted as soon as the Pilgrim fathers could clear the land, in 1648.

Both garlic and leeks were already domesticated by the time early civilizations were developing their first forms of writing. Leeks, like onions, were valued as food, but garlic was less readily accepted, perhaps because of its greater pungency. As soon as onions were cultivated, so, too, were garlic and leeks.

As to other members of the onion family—scallions, shallots, and chives—they were depicted in early forms of art, but rarely mentioned in writing. Shallots, indeed, have a shadowy history. They were probably first recognized in the twelfth or thirteenth century. For a time, they were thought to have come from Ascalon, a city in Judea. Pliny the Elder (A.D. 23 to 79) started this theory by misinterpreting a sentence by Theophrastus; Pliny saw the word *askalonian* and thought it was a reference to shallots. In *Food*, Waverley Root sets the record straight: " . . . *askalonian* does not appear to have derived from *Askalon*."

Some botanists deny that the shallot ever grew wild, claiming it is descended from the common onion. On the other hand, chives may always have been wild. The history of this grassy, aromatic plant is even sketchier than the documentation for shallots. There does seem to be evidence that wild chives were common in ancient

Greece and Italy. Unlike most of the other alliums, however, chives do not seem to have been domesticated. Perhaps they were simply plucked from the ground in their wild state, to be eaten raw and/or used for medicinal purposes. That may be why they rarely appear in the otherwise full and vivid history of the onion family.

THE MEANING OF THE ONION

Barter

Can you imagine paying your taxes in garlic? Until the middle of the eighteenth century, the tax collector in Siberia was paid in just this manner. According to the Fresh Garlic Association, in ancient Egypt, an aristocrat could buy a "healthy" male slave for fifteen pounds of garlic. Leeks, as well, were legal tender in some places. As evidence suggests, alliums were not only a staple of ancient diets, but also a form of coin.

Literature

References to the onion and its relatives can be found in many literatures, and certainly in the Bible. In Numbers 11:5, the children of Israel lament the meager desert diet enforced by the exodus: "We remember the fish, which we did eat in Egypt freely; the cucumbers, and the melons, and the leeks, and the onions, and the garlic." In Renaissance England, the associations were more figurative—at least in Shakespeare's *Coriolanus*. A noble Roman refers to the mob of tradesmen as "garlic-eaters" (act IV; scene vi; line 99), an allusion to their working-class status.

Folk Medicine

Throughout history, in many parts of Europe, especially in Eastern Europe and the Balkan countries, people believed that diseases like the plague were caused by evil spirits. Onions, and particularly garlic, were employed to cast spells, act as good luck charms, ward off the "evil eye," and chase off evil spirits. According to popular belief, the pungent cloves had power over other agents of the Devil, as well. Garlic was hung on the windows and doors of homes, and strings of garlic were worn around the neck to keep vampires at bay. This charm also had power over more earthly assailants: bullfighters in Spain would carry cloves into the ring to prevent the bull from charging.

While garlic was used to prevent harm, it was also used to procure happiness. Hans Licht, author of *Sexual Life in Ancient Greece*, writes: "The onion is the most frequently named among Greek erotic stimulants." Some historians believe this association may have inspired the Thracian custom of giving onions as wedding gifts. Even now in the Middle East, often a clove of garlic is worn in the buttonhole of a bridegroom's wedding suit to ensure a happy wedding night.

Still, attitudes toward garlic have been ambivalent. More than any other member of the onion family, garlic has aroused the passions of the people, who have simultaneously worshiped it for its God-like powers and rejected it as an aid to the Devil. The mistrust of garlic, and sometimes of onions, may have come not only from their strong scent and taste, but from certain stories passed on from generation to generation. For example, according to ancient Turkish legend, the onion was born when Satan was cast out of Paradise. It sprouted where his right foot touched earth, while garlic sprang up under his left foot.

Overwhelmingly, however, alliums have been valued for their health-giving properties. Very often, there's a fine line between superstition and folk medicine. Onions and garlic were used to heal everything from plague and scurvy to burns, bee stings, and athlete's foot. Before gathering a particularly poisonous root, Greek root gatherers would rub themselves with garlic oil or eat a lot of garlic to protect themselves from the juices—or even the aura—of the deadly plant. In Rome, alliums were high on the list of medicinal remedies. Pliny the Elder (A.D. 23 to 79), the Roman naturalist, wrote a myriad of remedies using alliums, sixty-one with garlic, and thirty-two with leeks. Indeed, the Emperor Nero, was nicknamed Porrophagus, or "leek eater," because he ate leeks several days each month to improve his voice. Leek syrup has been recommended even in our own time, as a home remedy for coughing and even for whooping cough. Chives, so often overlooked, have some virtues, too. In Chinese folk medicine, chives were used as an antidote to poison.

Given the long history and varied uses of alliums, it is not surprising that anecdotes abound. Alexander the Great believed onions restored courage and so fed large quantities of them to his armies. During the Civil War, General Ulysses S. Grant used onion juice as an antiseptic to clean wounds; however, he may have had Alexander in mind when he wrote to the war department: "I will not move my troops without onions." He received three cartloads. Much later, Eleanor Roosevelt would make her own pitch for alliums. Her superior memory and energy, she said, could be attributed to her daily ritual of taking exercise, vitamins, and three chocolate-covered garlic pills.

Today, the value of onions can be empirically documented. And, it turns out, onions are good for you! The bulb onion is low in calories—1 medium onion contains only 38 calories—and high in flavor. A boon to dieters, onions add flavor to "diet" food without adding unwanted calories. Onions are also high in fiber ($\frac{1}{2}$ cup cooked onions contains 1.6 grams fiber). That too is good news for those trying to lose weight: A meal that's rich in fiber tends to fill you up sooner, so that you don't eat as much. Fiber also reduces fat absorption during digestion. When you eat an onion, you are also getting essential minerals, important vitamins, and carbohydrates.

Many of the old home remedies are still being used throughout the world, and many of the old superstitions are turning out to be well founded. Investigation shows that the eating of onions may help prevent not only the common cold but also more serious ailments. Raw onions, when chewed for a short time, act as a strong antibacterial and antiviral instrument, sterilizing the mouth and throat. In this way, they may be useful against digestive ailments and lung infections.

Moreover, alliums may be effective against some of the most common, talked-about current threats to our health. The oils of onions and garlic contain sulfur, which when eaten in large quantities may impede cancer in its very early stages. Alliums also contain a chemical called Prostaglandin A_1, an agent that reduces blood pressure. Alliums also have a cholesterol-lowering effect and can increase HDL (high-density lipoprotein), a substance that may hinder dangerous blood clotting. All these contribute to a healthy heart and circulatory system. Eventually, we may come to know whether it is better to eat alliums raw or cooked and in what quantity for optimal benefit. Until then, however, we appreciate every member of the onion family, different as they all are, for their unique and captivating qualities.

CHAPTER TWO

Understanding Onions

While only a few of the hundreds of species in the genus *Alliaceae* have made it into cultivation either as food or as flower, there are thousands of "varieties" of onions produced commercially around the world. They come in various shapes, sizes, and skin colors, ranging from the marble-sized, dainty white pearl onion to the globular all-purpose yellow onion to the spindle-shaped, bronzy, pink-red Florence onion. In terms of the market-place, onions can weigh anywhere from an ounce, called a "baby," up to a pound, called a "colossal." Though there are only three basic skin colors—yellow, white, and red—there are many variable hues of each. The intensity of their flavor runs the gamut from pungent to sweet and from mild to hot and spicy. Even subtle variations of soil, climate, and weather conditions can significantly affect the flavor of onions. So, not surprisingly, the same seed variety grown in the same place can result in produce that differs from year to year. One day you could buy a storage onion and it might be mild, with just a slight bite, and the next day you could purchase the same onion, but from a new shipment, at the same greengrocer's and it might be strong in flavor—almost hot.

Understanding onions is difficult not only because of the large number of varieties and many varietal names, but because of the nuances among some of the varieties. All this makes a well-informed onion purchase in the market all the more difficult and even more important that the buyer "know his or her onions." Yet, and in spite of the confusion over the names, be they common or specific, onions can be grouped into several general categories, simply for practical purposes of understanding.

Basically onions are divided: the **dry bulb onion** and the **green onion.** Division is based on the onion's growing region(s), harvesting time, seed variety, and bulb formation. The dry bulb category is broken down even further into the fresh onion and the storage onion types. Onions reach these subcategories depending on seed variety, when they are harvested, and for how long they are cured. There are three general ways of curing. One is when the onions sit several weeks in burlap bags in the field. Another way is to bring the onions indoors and use a heat process to cure them. The third way is to gently dig up the plants, pull to the earth surface, and let them sit in the field for several weeks, allowing the elements to cure them.

Dry Bulb Onions: Fresh Onions

Fresh onions are so named because they are "freshly picked" and must be used within several weeks of purchase. Their skin color tends to be on the light side and their skin quite thin—tissue-like. They are available from the end of March until late August.

The distinctive charm of the fresh onion is its exceptionally sweet, mild taste and crisp, juicy texture due to its higher water and sugar content. The popular Vidalia onion has a 12.5 percent natural sugar content. (Compare this to an apple with 11 percent natural sugar content.) A fresh onion contains about 35 percent water compared to a storage onion, the water content of which ranges from 8 to 10 percent. And, if the fresh onion is cured, which it sometimes is, an even sweeter taste results. Specialty fresh onions that can be purchased in the United States include such regional favorites as Hawaii's Maui, Georgia's Vidalia, Washington's Walla Walla, and Texas's 1015 SuperSweet. Keep in mind that naming onions by the region in which they are grown is somewhat fueled by promotional marketing strategies, and is not true of all onion classification.

It is important to note here before going on to storage onions that the term *fresh* can sometimes be confusing because you can buy a fresh onion that has been picked and sold soon thereafter such as a spring green onion (see page 20) and you can buy a fresh onion that has been cured (dried out) for up to a week. The distinction between the two, besides flavor, resides in the difference in appearance. The skin of an onion picked and sold soon thereafter will be thin and wet. The skin of a cured onion will also be thin, but dry and tight, resembling a storage onion.

DRY BULB ONIONS: STORAGE ONIONS

Storage onions are so named because of their ability to store well over the winter months. Storage onions are harvested beginning in August, then cured for at least a week and then they are sold. Or, if the intent is to "store" them for later use, they are harvested in September, cured for at least a week, and put into storage. The curing process results in a dry, papery skin on the onion (darker and thicker than that of the fresh onion's) that protects onions during shipping and holding and helps prevent decay. Storage onions such as the all-purpose yellow onion are available in the market beginning in August—just as the fresh onion season is coming to an end—and are available throughout the winter months until late March. Most of the onions eaten in North America are storage onions.

The more obvious distinction between fresh onions and storage onions lies in their water content. Because the water content of storage onions is lower than that of fresh onions, storage onions do not seem as juicy, generally have a more pungent flavor, and store better.

Before I go any further I think now would be a good time to explain the reason for the number of varieties of both fruits and vegetables, especially onions, available to the consumer today. Simply put, it is hybridization. To explain briefly, some "varieties" evolve in nature, and some are bred for desired horticultural characteristics; these varieties are called "cultivars." Hybridization occurs when a seed breeder pollinates a specific variety (or cultivar) with a different variety (or cultivar) as it comes into bloom, thus creating a new variety that combines the characteristics of both parents called a "hybrid." But, keep in mind that a hybrid can have multiple sets of parents. For example, in the United States most of the onions you see labeled Bermuda merely mimic the real Bermuda onion, because the original was mixed with other strains to create Bermuda "types." While these so-called types will have some of the original characteristics of the Bermuda onion, the original was discontinued approximately eight years ago. Communication breakdown is the reason the Bermuda label on these onions has kept on in the United States. However, Bermuda onions are still available in Caribbean countries. There are many reasons for hybridization, such as the attempt to produce new disease-resistant varieties, or varieties that are more specific to consumers' needs, or those that are better for storage and yield more abundantly. In the case of the Bermuda onion it was initiated by "selective breeding." After being used for a number of years, a genetic line is weakened. So, breeders replace it with other genetic parentage that produces better, more consistent results that a grower looks for and a consumer appreciates. In other words, there can be as many different onion varieties as seed breeders have combinations; the number of varieties is dictated by the needs of the grower and consumer.

GREEN ONIONS

Green onions include spring green onions, scallions, chives, leeks, and Welsh onions. Green onions are generally considered a subcategory of fresh onions, but I prefer to think of them as a separate category altogether.

Spring green onions are the young, immature bulbs of almost any onion type; sometimes they are a scallion variety that has been allowed more time in the ground. They are harvested when their tops are green and tender and just before the underground bulb has fully developed. Typically, these onions are white, marble-sized bulbs with green veins and very thin, transparent skin, and they are not cured.

Sold in bunches with their tubular greens still attached in the produce section of most supermarkets, spring green onions are entirely edible, including their leaves. They have a mild, clean, crisp flavor and texture and are delicious raw or cut up and served in a salad. They should be used as soon as possible or stored in the refrigerator, where they should keep at least three days. Their peak season is from May through June.

Scallions are onion seeds that are planted as soon as their seeds germinate. Then their growth is abruptly halted by pulling at the green stage and bunched before the base has begun to swell into a bulb shape.

However, most often, scallions are grown from "nonbulbing" onion seed varieties so farmers don't have to be as careful as to when they pull them. Farmers also plant them densely so the onions are crowded and growth is slowed down. Scallions can also make onion "sets"—young plants that have already germinated and are ready for transplanting. These sets can be sold the following spring as the first stage in growing onion bulbs.

Oftentimes, scallions are incorrectly called by such names as spring onions or shallots. Yet, they are all very different, with different tastes especially. Please turn to Chapter 3 to learn more about the green onion members.

Spring Green Onions

GARLIC

Though garlic has a distinctly different taste from onions, they are related. There are many varieties of it. To make matters more confusing, their common names are not standardized. The garlic plant (*Allium sativum*) has flat, grayish green leaves with stalks bearing delicate, white flowers. The part of the plant so revered is the bulb, more commonly referred to as the "head." Each finger section is called a "clove." Garlic skin varies in color from white to yellow to dark purple, and the clove shape varies from long and slender to short and fat. Garlic can range in taste from warm and sweet to hot and pungent. And as with the other allium species, even within an individual garlic strain there can be substantial differences in flavor and potency. The garlic typically available to consumers year round has been harvested and cured. Surprisingly, it is termed "fresh." However, there is garlic that can also be eaten as a young plant, and it, too, is often referred to as "fresh," "green," or "wet." This garlic is sold soon after harvesting and is not cured or dried. It has light flavor with juicy cloves, since it hasn't been cured—the process that removes excess moisture—thereby intensifying the flavor and aroma. Usually, green garlic can be purchased in the spring at a farmers' market or specialty grocery store though you can grow your own.

Garlic

According to Ron L. Engeland in *Growing Great Garlic,* garlic is divided into two subspecies: hardneck and softneck. Hardneck garlic is considered a gourmet delicacy. It has fewer and larger cloves, which peel quite easily, but does not store well. Rocambole and serpent garlic are examples of hardneck garlic. Softneck garlic does not peel easily, but stores much better and longer than does its hardneck counterpart. Artichoke garlic is a softneck garlic.

HEIRLOOM ONIONS: ONIONS WITH A PAST

Heirloom onions are prized for their unusually fine flavors and for the variety of their colors and shapes. Most heirloom varieties have been passed down from one generation of immigrants to the next.

For the most part, heirloom varieties of produce are grown in home gardens. Heirloom seeds are typically open-pollinated; some are pollinated by the wind or insects; and some are self-pollinating, unlike the hybrid seeds of today. Because these seeds are open-pollinated, they can be saved and used year after year, and the results are consistent. The seeds of modern hybrids, on the other hand, cannot be saved; some are sterile, and even if they do save and grow, next year's crop will not resemble the current one. Hybrid seeds must, therefore, be purchased afresh each year.

For further information on where to buy heirloom onion seeds such as the Wethersfield onion or the purple queen onion, please see page 176. The Seed Savers Exchange, for one, is an organization whose members work toward saving heirloom and endangered food crops from extinction.

WILD ONIONS

Euell Gibbons writes in his book *Stalking the Wild Asparagus,* "America is blessed with many kinds of wild onions. They are one of the most abundant and widespread of all wild food plants, one or more species being found in every state from the Atlantic to the

Pacific, and from Canada to Mexico." The following list includes some of the more commonly found and tastier of the numerous wild onions available. Should this inspire you to forage for wild onions, before you do please consult a field guide for specific technical information and illustrations, so that any confusion between edible and nonedible—potentially toxic—will be avoided. Also, consider the areas you choose to forage and make sure it is legal to pick there.

Meadow Garlic/Wild Shallot (Allium canadense)

This is often referred to as "wild garlic." Tiny bulblets create a spherical cluster of "top bulbs" that grow at the end of this thin seed stalk with long, tubular-shaped leaves. Each "top bulb" contains several dozen miniature bulbs that look like fat garlic cloves. Meadow garlic can be found growing in rich soil—typically low meadows—from New Jersey to Florida and west to the Great Plains.

Wild garlic should be gathered just like scallions, in bunches. You can clean and chop the tender inner leaves and use them to add zest in stews or casseroles. Do not use the tough outer layers of leaves. Traditionally, the clusters of top bulbs are gathered up before they are ripe so they don't break apart and are then pickled. The underground bulbs can be cleaned of all dirt, then parboiled, then sautéed in butter and/or olive oil until tender, and served hot. Or they can be boiled until tender, about half an hour, seasoned, and served hot. If you decide to boil them, be sure to reserve the cooking water as a base for delectable onion soup.

Nodding Wild Onion/Little Prairie Onion/Lady's Leek (Allium cernuum)

These wild onions are bell-shaped and subtly scented, and have white, pink, or purple-colored pendulous flowers in an umbel at the tip of a six- to eighteen-inch flower scape, which is bent back near the top to look as if nodding—hence the name. They like full sun and are commonly found from New York to South Carolina. The underground bulbs have strong flavor and can be served as a vegetable. Simply clean them, boil for about half an hour until crisp-tender, then drain. Return the bulbs to the same pot with water to cover, and simmer until tender. Season and serve hot. These bulbs are also good pickled.

Ramp/Wild Leek (Allium tricoccum)

Ramps have large, wide, flat, dark green leaves that are almost lance-shaped with a slender, firm, white bulb at the base. They have a strong scent and hearty onion flavor; in fact, they are the strongest scented of all the onion tribe. These onions can be found in moist, wooded areas with rich soils such as in the Appalachian Mountains. You can also find them from southern Quebec through New England, as far west as Minnesota, and as far south as Georgia. Nowadays during the spring, ramps are sold at many farmers' markets.

Ramps are best cooked soon after picking because their strong

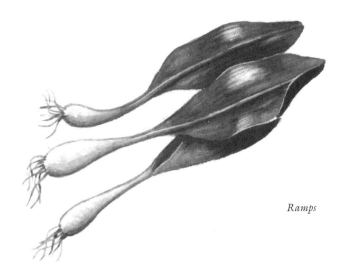

Ramps

aroma can penetrate other foods if you choose to store them. Both bulb and leaves can be used as a vegetable and seasoning. They should be cooked and can even be deep-fried. Enjoy them as a side dish or mixed with other ingredients such as potatoes. When I went to the Cosby Tennessee Ramp Festival, I tasted them in scrambled eggs. If you are going to store ramps, wrap them loosely in moistened paper towels and place them inside an unsealed plastic bag. If using a perforated plastic vegetable bag, seal it. Either way, store in the vegetable drawer of your refrigerator up to three days.

ORNAMENTAL ONIONS

As mentioned earlier, the genus *Alliaceae* encompasses around 500 species and each species can be subdivided into hundreds of varieties. This genus includes not only pasture and lawn weeds, essential food and medicinal plants, but there are also onions grown for their flowers! These stupendous onions are not edible (though there are a few exceptions), but are for show—a garden landscape or floral arrangement be it fresh or dried. Ornamental onions come in virtually every color except true red. Their size ranges from ankle to shoulder height, and many of them have a lovely fragrance. However, if they are bruised they smell oniony; and when they are dried they lose their smell completely.

Among those best used fresh are the *Allium cernuum,* with its lightly scented florets of pink, purple, or white, and the *Allium schubertii,* with its rose-pink flowers, both great for the garden or a floral arrangement. You also might find the *Allium giganteum*—tall four- to five-feet-high stalks bursting with five-inch-wide amethyst-colored balls—at your local flower shop or the *Allium schoenoprasum*—small, pinkish-purple orbs with grasslike leaves. One of the best onions for drying is *Allium albopilosum,* more commonly referred to as the star of Persia. It grows to be about one and one half to two and one half inches high with a six- to twelve-inch spherical head comprising starry, lavender flowers with a metallic sheen. For further information about where you can purchase some of the more common flowering onions, see Resources, page 173. You will be pleasantly surprised at what you find!

Allium Giganteum

CHAPTER THREE

An Onion Sampler

There are so many varieties of onions it would be impossible for me to chronicle all of them in this small book. I have, therefore, chosen to discuss the basic onion species and provide a sampling of their varieties. Below you will find their general characteristics—size, shape, color, and flavor—their seasonal availability, tips on what to look for, how to store them, and how to prepare them. Because botanists often disagree on the "correct" classifications of species in the *allium* genus, I have also included the Latin names as a guide to the many alliums available. (In addition, at the end of this volume there is an appendix, which lists mail-order companies that offer cuttings, plants, or seeds to grow your own onions at home.)

Before you begin cooking any type of onion, you should ask yourself the following questions to determine if you have chosen the appropriate onion for your recipe.

- Is this onion in season; if not, can I substitute another?
- Do I want an onion with a mild, sweet flavor or one with a strong bite, almost hot?
- What about presentation? Do I need an onion of a certain size? with color?
- Do I want to cook this onion? or is it better raw?
- Can this onion can stored for a few days? or must I use it right away?
- Am I using this onion to its fullest capacity?

CHIVES
(Allium schoenoprasum)

Common green chives are the most delicate and subtly flavored members of the onion family. Sweet with a peppery overtone, but no hint of heat, they are perennials, with waif-like, tubular leaves and purple flowers that are edible when pesticide-free and have a delicious, delicate onion taste. Chives are sold in bunches and are available year round. Know that chives do not form underground bulbs.

Garlic chives/Oriental garlic chives/Chinese chives/Chinese leeks—four different names for the same plant—are perennial herbs, each with crunchy, flat, dark green, narrow grasslike leaves, although a broad-leaf type also exists that can be used in place of garlic for flavor. White blossoms appear in late summer and are edible when pesticide-free. Use the leaves like chives and mince the bulbs and use them as garlic.

Worth mentioning here are the Chinese leek flower and yellow Chinese chives, a deviation of Chinese chives. Blanched yellow by having soil mounded around their leaves in the garden, these chives are just now beginning to reach farmers' markets in the United States, where the demand is so high. They can also fre-

Chinese Leek Flowers

quently be purchased at better Oriental markets. The Chinese leek flower is popular in the Orient for its flowers, which have an unusual hearty, leek-like flavor. The flowers, which begin to appear in the spring, are harvested at the bud stage.

The Market and the Cook

When purchasing chives, choose small bundles of unblemished, bright green unwithered stalks, not yellow or slimy ones. The lavender-colored fluffy blossoms, if attached, are also edible when pesticide-free.

To store: Loosely wrap chives in damp paper towels and place in an unsealed plastic bag. If using a perforated plastic vegetable bag, seal it. Store in the vegetable drawer of the refrigerator up to three days. Use as soon as possible; the longer chives sit, the less flavorful they become. Chives are best used just after being snipped or purchased.

If using the flowers of Chinese leeks or the Chinese leek flower strain, pick tightly closed buds, because as the flower opens and the plant matures, the stalks become woody and tough. Cook the flowers still attached to the tender stalks as a side dish.

Recipe match   Use chives whenever a hint of sweet onion flavor is needed; for example, snipped, they make a delicious addition to potato salad or scrambled eggs. The leaves of Chinese chives, specifically, tend to have a rougher texture than ordinary chive leaves, so they need to be finely chopped. Chinese chives are great stir-fried or added to a dumpling filling. In general, though, chives are best when used raw because their flavor lessens when cooked.

Cooking basics   Snip chives with kitchen scissors for best results, or use a very sharp knife in quick, even slicing strokes. Do not crush or the flavorful juice will be lost. If using in a cooked dish, add chives at the very last minute, so as not to destroy their delicate flavor and tender texture. Be careful not to overcook Oriental chives, in particular, because they will get stringy and tasteless.

GARLIC
(Allium sativum)

Artichoke garlic are the most commonly available and popular garlics in the United States and are considered all-purpose garlics. The bulbs are often large, dull in color, and somewhat rough or lumpy in appearance. With several layers of irregularly shaped cloves, the largest form on the outer layer. Often called "Italian" garlic, these are good storing bulbs. The taste varies widely from mild to hot.

Elephant garlic produces bulbs with large cloves and can weigh, on the average, about eight ounces per bulb, but has been known to get up to one pound. In flavor and shape, elephant garlic resembles regular garlic, although in flavor it is milder, with less aromatic oil. Raw, it has bite. Cooked, it is milder in flavor. It is also good for cooking because its larger cloves are easier to peel.

Rocambol/ophioscorodon/serpent garlic have the strongest flavor of any garlics. A purple-blotched bulb, which produces cloves in a single circle, they have the shortest storage time, so make sure that the bulbs are firm when you buy them. The coiled shape of the tall, looping garlic stem gives this plant its common name—serpent garlic—which is the literal translation of the Greek name "ophioscorodon."

The Market and the Cook

When buying garlic, choose plump, firm bulbs with tissue-paper-like skin that is not peeling, flaking, or stained. Stay away from bulbs that are soft, spongy, or shriveled as they will be dry and bitter with much less flavor. Avoid bulbs that are sprouting. In addition, no strong odor should be obvious; it can mean sprouting has begun.

A whole bulb should last from one to eight weeks, depending on its age and condition when purchased, as well as the storage conditions. Cloves will keep two to ten days. Once a clove is peeled, use it the same day, preferably at once; it does not store well after being peeled.

To store: Put garlic in a dry, well-ventilated place, away from heat, moisture, and light. Do not refrigerate or freeze. Do not store in plastic; moisture causes garlic to mold. I suggest purchasing a garlic cellar—a small clay pot with holes and a lid—made just for storing garlic.

Braided garlic can be hung from a hook, in a cool, dry place. The braid helps garlic last longer, for about two months.

Recipe match Elephant garlic is excellent raw in salads or cooked whole in soups. Its unopened flower buds can be sautéed and combined with other vegetables, rice, or couscous to make a tasty side dish.

Cooking basics To peel garlic: Lay a damp kitchen towel under a cutting board to prevent it from slipping. Place the clove of garlic on the cutting board and using the heel of your hand carefully press the flat side of a wide knife blade down on the clove to split the skin. With your fingers, peel off the skin and cut off the root end and any brown spots on the clove.

To peel several heads of garlic at once: Drop the separated, trimmed cloves into boiling water for 20 seconds, drain, then pinch each clove at one end; the peel should slip off easily. Garlic when it is cooked like this will lose a little of its flavor. Note: Do not put garlic or onion peels down your drain; they will clog it.

When garlic is crushed through a garlic press, it reaches its maximum potency; minced garlic is about five to ten times weaker than crushed garlic. Simply press halved but unpeeled garlic cloves in a garlic press. After pressing garlic, discard solids left behind and wash and dry press.

To mellow garlic flavor: Before using, boil peeled garlic cloves for five minutes.

To prevent a bitter garlic flavor: Using a sharp paring knife, peel and cut clove in half lengthwise, and remove any bitter green shoot, if present, from the center of clove.

These onions, also known as **Chinese bunching onions/Welsh onions/winter onions/French** *ciboules* (*Allium fistulosum*), are used mostly in Chinese and Japanese dishes and are grown all over the Far East. In America we refer to them as Welsh onions, while the Germans call them winter onions, and the French *ciboules*. In appearance they are a little larger than scallions, with root ends that are slightly swollen, not straight like the one on a scallion. The leaves are round and hollow. They are a nonbulbing variety that is occasionally used to grow scallions in America. While they may resemble scallions somewhat, in flavor they are more similar to leeks.

The Market and the Cook

Occasionally you will see these onions in American supermarkets or at farmers' markets, but they tend to be labeled "leeks" and not "Japanese bunching onions" or any of the other names they go by such as the "evergreen" or "perennial onion." They are great for the home garden because of their hardiness and ability to form clumps, which can be dug up at any time and used in dishes just as scallions are. They can also be grown in a container such as a window box.

To store: Wrap loosely in plastic wrap and store in the vegetable drawer of the refrigerator for three to five days.

Recipe match These onions are best used raw as they tend to get limp and lose flavor when cooked. However, they do work well when added to a hot dish, or soup or broth like *miso* just before serving.

Cooking basics Treat as you would scallions.

LEEKS
(Allium Porrum)

Leeks are grown from leek seeds and, unlike onions, do not grow bulbs. As the plants mature, soil should be piled around them so that the stalks are protected from sunlight and remain white. Leeks range in size from thin to thick and have broad, flat, green leaves that form a chevron pattern on the stalks. The size and age of the leek will greatly affect the flavor of any recipe in which it is used.

American large flag leeks are noteworthy for their blue-green leaves that tend to recurve and their somewhat short stalks. Giant Musselburgh leeks, another common variety, are larger, nine to fifteen inches tall and two to three inches in diameter, have medium to dark green, fan-shaped leaves, and tender stalks.

The Market and the Cook

When purchasing leeks, look for slender ones, about one and a half to two inches in diameter, with fresh green tops and smooth, unblemished white bases. Leeks should also be flexible to the touch; if not, chances are that they will have an unappealing, woody texture. Peak seasons for leeks is fall, winter, and spring; a well-stocked store carries them year round.

To store: Wrap leeks loosely in plastic wrap and place in the vegetable drawer of the refrigerator for three to five days.

Recipe match Leek varieties can be used interchangeably. Though there are flavor differences among them, neither the change in flavor nor texture is dramatic. The soothing oniony flavor of leeks makes wonderful soups and fillings for savory pastries or quiches and can always be served whole and hot as a side dish with vinaigrette or cream sauce. Leeks are not eaten raw because the flavor is hot and somewhat bitter. But what is most unappealing is the tough, chewy texture. However, when cooked, their texture is almost buttery.

Cooking basics When cooked, leeks have a smooth texture similar to that of asparagus, and, in fact, the French often refer to them as the "poor man's asparagus."

Generally, only the white part of leeks is used; the flat, green tops of the leaves being too coarse for most recipes. Don't discard these, though—save them to flavor soup or stocks. Indeed, leeks are known as the "king of the soup onion."

Unfortunately, leeks are difficult to clean, with sand and dirt wedged between the many leaf layers. To prepare for cooking, trim away the roots and cut off the green tops at the point where the white bulb turns light green in color. Remove any tough outer leaves. Split the stalk lengthwise to cut in half, then wash carefully under cold running water to remove any sand, but try to keep the leek from falling apart. If you need to leave the leeks whole, make a slit down the center but not through, and rinse under running water while using your fingers to fan the leaves open slightly so the water can rinse away the sand.

Bulb Onions
(Allium cepa)

All-purpose yellow onions are typically chosen most often for cooking. They are globe-shaped, golden-yellow-skinned onions with a medium to strong taste that at times can also be hot. Their shape and pungency can differ, depending on the time of year. An all-purpose yellow can weigh as little as an ounce or as much as one pound.

This onion is available throughout the year. From March through September the skins are thinner, and the onions have a higher water and sugar content. At this time they are typically milder in flavor. Because they do not store as well, they need to be eaten soon after being purchased. From September to March, these onions have thicker skins and tend to be harder and heavier. Their flavor ranges from mildly pungent to hot. At this time, when sold in bulk those onions which are larger in size can have less pungency.

Boiling onions are grown in the same manner as pearl onions, but because they are intended to be larger—about one and one half inches in diameter—they are simply planted a little further apart. Boiling onions are golf ball size, somewhat egg-shaped, with white skin. However, reddish-purple skin and yellow skin boiling onions are sometimes also available.

California Sweet Imperials are globe-shaped, yellow-skinned onions with meaty rings, and are seasonal. They are sweet and succulent with a subtle onion flavor. They tend to be marketed when approximately two and one half inches in diameter but are available in medium, large, and colossal sizes. They are grown in California's Imperial Valley and are only available from April to June.

Carzalia onions are round, with a slightly flattened top, light yellow-skinned, sweet seasonal onions. They are marketed when about three to three and one half inches in diameter. They are available from June through August.

Catawissa or **walking onions** are very similar, virtually identical, to the Egyptian top onion, which forms a cluster of sets on the tip of its stalk and also divides underground to provide underground bulbs. These onions got the name "walking onions" from the way in which the mature stalks fall to the ground, allowing the cluster of sets to take root some distance from the parent. Presently, these onions are not sold in the marketplace, but can be grown at home.

Cipolline (pronounced chi-po-li-nee) are imported from Italy and nicknamed Italian button onions. Small, sphere-shaped onions with pearly white to yellowish-bronze paper-thin skins and firm, fine-grained flesh, they have a well-developed flavor that is slightly sweet. They are about one to two inches in diameter and both ends are characteristically flat.

Cipolline

Cocktail onions are simply pickled baby pearl onions. They are sold in jars, packed in brine, and can be found in almost any supermarket.

Dehydrated onions can be found in the spice and seasoning sections of many supermarkets in the following forms: powdered, granulated, ground, minced, chopped, and sliced. Onion salt, dehydrated garlic, powdered garlic, and garlic salt are also available in these departments. I do not recommend using them as a substitute for fresh onions or garlic.

Egyptian top onions/tree onions (*A. cepa var. viviparum*) are a topset onion that after flowering produces clusters of small, edible bulbils on the ends of tubular shoots—hence its name. These onions can grow anywhere from twelve inches to two feet high and if not harvested immediately, the weight will cause the shoots to fall over and take root. In the spring, the tender young shoots can be used like scallions. These onions also divide at the base to form a clump of very hardy onions, so you never have to dig or replant. Fresh green onions will sprout from the clump in the fall, and again in the spring. At the time of publication these onions are not sold in the marketplace, but you can grow them at home.

Egyptian Top Onions/Tree Onions

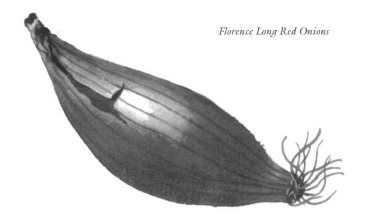

Florence Long Red Onions

Florence long red onions are bottle- or spindle-shaped onion bulbs that grow to be about six inches long. They have purple-red skin, a mild sweet flavor that can be on the spicy-tangy side, and light red flesh. I have found that these bulbs are sometimes called "torpedo" onions in farmers' markets, even though there is another variety by this same name. Presently, it is unlikely that you can find these onions in the marketplace other than in some areas of California, during the summer and fall. However, you can grow them in a home garden.

Fresno Sweets are glossy, deep burgundy-wine red-skinned onions, with a sweet flavor and medium pungency, and dense, solid flesh. They are marketed in medium- to large-sized bulbs that are flat at both ends and when sliced have thick purplish-red rings. They are available from mid-May through August.

Frozen chopped onions are available in your grocer's freezer. When in a hurry, use as a substitute; they save time in both peeling and chopping.

Italian sweet red onions are dark reddish-purple-skinned onions with reddish-purple rimmed slices. Flat on both ends, they have a sweet, mild flavor, while their texture can be coarse, and are marketed in medium to large sizes. They are available March through September.

Italian Sweet Red Onions

Maui onions are grown in the volcanic soil of the mountains of Maui, Hawaii. They are round in shape, with flat tops and creamy white skin with a slight green to yellow cast. They have a distinctive sweet but mild onion flavor and are especially juicy. They are sold in various sizes: small, medium, large, and jumbo. Their peak season ranges from April through June, with limited supplies available from June through December.

Multiplier onions refer to a type of onion whose varieties grow much like that of potato onions, but they produce smaller bulbs. The aggregatum group (*Allium cepa var. aggregatum*) includes potato onions, multiplier onions, and shallots. With the exception of shallots, the group as a whole has become scarce in recent years, but is now gaining popularity due to their flavor through heirloom seed channels and by virtue of the fact that these onions can be grown as scallions or grown as small pearl-type onions. Like shallots and potato onions, multiplier onions also divide underground to form clusters of bulbs. Yellow multiplier onions so resemble shallots that they are sometimes sold by that name. The white multiplier onion is fairly rare; its chive-like leaves are very sweet and mild when harvested. Currently, they are not available in the marketplace, but you can grow them at home.

Nu-Mex Sweet onions are round with flat tops, slightly tapered bottoms, and pale yellow-gold skin, and are seasonal. They have a sweet, mild flavor and are available during the month of June.

Pearl onions are usually the result of a style of cultivation. They are not young onions but in fact mature onions. They are between one inch and one and one quarter inches in diameter. Farmers simply plant about three times as many of the seeds closer together, stunting the growth and keeping the bulb small. Another way of keeping the bulbs small is to grow a short-day or southern onion variety in a northern area, or vice versa. Though American pearl onions are simply almost any *Allium cepa* variety that has been kept to a small size by cultivation practices, there is a true "pearl onion" cultivated in Europe that can be found pickled and sold in jars in American specialty food stores. Specific varieties are chosen by farmers to yield firm-fleshed sweet onions. Marble-sized, globe-shaped, and slightly tapered, pearl onions have various skin colors. Typically, you see pearl onions during the winter holiday season, when they are sold in pint baskets. Frozen pearl onions are available in the freezer department of most supermarkets throughout the year, and are a very good substitute since they not only have good flavor but save you time in peeling.

Potato onions grow underground in a cluster, similar to how potatoes grow—hence the name. Both the bulbs and the greens are edible. Though red and white varieties are available through gardening supply catalogs, it is the yellow potato onion that is most common.

Spanish Sweet onions at one time were actually imported from Spain. Today they are raised in the United States. While red-skinned and white-skinned varieties are available, the dominant variety—yellow sweet Spanish—is known for its large size, spherical shape, mild, sweet flavor and crispness. At times they can have a little heat. The Idaho-Oregon production area calls their onions of this type "Spanish Sweets," which are available from August through March.

Texas 1015 SuperSweet Onions

Texas 1015 SuperSweet onions are seasonal onions, named for their recommended October 15 planting date. They are harvested in the Lower Rio Grande Valley and are available in the markets starting April through June. They are sweet, with no bite or sting, and are jumbo in size—like a softball—and round, with a very thin pale-yellow skin. This onion is known for its 90 percent single-center, meaning it has more rings.

Vidalia onions (pronounced vy–DALE–yuh) are also seasonal onions that are grown in a twenty-county area of Georgia that has been designated by state law and that has a unique microclimate with mild temperatures. Only those onions grown in those parts are allowed to be called "Vidalia onions." Vidalias are cultivated in sandy, sulfur-deficient soil; specific amounts of fertilizers help maintain the onion's sweet flavor. A light yellow–golden brown bulb that is rounded on the bottom and somewhat flat on the top, the Vidalia ranges in size from medium to large to jumbo. Available in late April through June, Vidalias are in limited supply in October and November, although some are stored in a low-oxygen environment.

Baby Vidalia onions are Vidalia onion plants that have been pulled from the fields before maturity, being harvested during the spring, with their greens still attached. They have not been cured

Vidalia Onions

or dried. In fact, the golf-ball-sized bulbs are generally available only through mail order (unless you grow them) in December and the early spring and are shipped overnight or second-day delivery. See Resources, page 173.

Walla Walla Sweets are grown primarily in the Walla Walla Valley in southeastern Washington state and are seasonal. Very sweet and juicy with thick layers of crunchy white flesh, Walla Wallas are round, with light yellow skin. Available in small, medium, large, and jumbo sizes, they appear in markets from mid-June through mid-August.

Walla Walla Sweets

White onions are smallish to medium-sized globe-shaped onions, about two to four inches in diameter, with white skin. They have a sharp flavor, strong bite, and can be typically hotter than the all-purpose yellow onion; they are generally the most pungent of the onions presently being sold in the United States marketplace, as they are bred, in fact, for their pungency. They tend to have a shorter shelf life than the all-purpose yellow onions because they contain proportionally more water. They are available year round, and during the spring are imported from Mexico, where pungent onions are a favorite.

ONION BREATH?

Cooked onions do not affect the breath, but raw onions and both cooked and fresh garlic do. Here are some easy solutions:

- Eat a sprig or two of fresh parsley; it is a natural breath freshener.
- Wash your mouth out with a rinse of equal amounts of fresh lemon juice and water.
- Eat an apple.

The Market and the Cook

When purchasing bulb onions, look for dry, firm, compact bulbs with shiny, blemish-free skin and tight, dry necks. If the bulb or neck is soft or wet and if sprouting has started, it is a sign that the onion has begun to rot. The skin should not show any signs of mold, and the flesh should be void of any brown areas, cuts, or bruises. The scent should not be overpowering, as this also suggests the onion is probably bruised.

To store storage onions: Keep in a well-ventilated, cool, dry, dark place. Do not store them piled, but in a single layer. Under such conditions, they will keep approximately four to five weeks. You can also store them in the legs of old, sheer clean pantyhose or stockings; place an onion carefully in the pantyhose, and tie a knot between each onion; hang in a cool, well-ventilated place, such as a cellar or garage. As you need one, cut off the bottom onion just above the knot. A wire egg basket hung in a cool, dark place is also a good container for storing onions. Keep onions away from direct sunlight, which will stimulate the production of chlorophyll and, since the layers of an onion are swollen leaf bases, will turn the flesh green and the taste bitter. And always keep onions away from potatoes, or the onions may get moldy. Braided onions can be hung from a hook, in a cool, dry place.

To store fresh onions: Keep in the refrigerator for one to three weeks. If they begin to sprout, they have been stored too long. I do not recommend freezing either fresh or storage onions because both the texture and flavor alter dramatically. Commercially frozen onions use a process that retains the onion's original qualities far more effectively.

Many specialty fresh onions are available in a variety of sizes—medium (two to three and one half inches in diameter), jumbo or large (three inches or more in diameter), and extra-large or colossal (four inches or larger in diameter). These sweet fresh onions are best raw.

If you do cook them, do so for only a short amount of time, until just crisp-tender, and they will maintain their shape. They may lose flavor, however. Be careful when adding them to an item containing bread, as the higher water content of a fresh onion might adversely affect the final product.

NUTRITIONAL REASONS
for Being an Onion Eater

Storage onions are relatively low in calories, at about 30 per $\frac{1}{2}$ cup. They are also low in sodium and have no fat or cholesterol. They provide a generous amount of folic acid, contain a surprising amount of vitamin C, twice as much as an apple, and are high in fiber (one medium onion contains 2.7 grams of dietary fiber). Lastly, they provide vitamin B_6, potassium, and other important vitamins and minerals.

Recipe match **All-purpose yellow onions** are just that: all-purpose. They are good in any raw or cooked dish in which onion flavor is the goal; though typically not as hot or as sharp as a white onion, they are also not as subtly flavored as a specialty sweet fresh onion. They are, in essence, "all-purpose"—well suited to a variety of uses. They can cook for hours because their texture and flavor remain intact though any heat disappears. They are also great for stuffing because when hollowed out there is enough room for a good-sized serving of filling *and* they do not fall apart when baked.

Boiling onions are best left whole and are superb in casseroles because they also hold their shape and flavor. And they are good boiled or simmered in stews.

California Sweet Imperials are wonderful coated with batter and deep-fried, because the cooking time is brief and batter protects the easily wilted sweet onion flesh. They are also good on the grill because grilling intensifies their natural sweetness.

Carzalia onions add sweetness to baked goods.

Catawissa onions and **Egyptian top onions'** cylindrical greens can be eaten raw or stuffed. The stalks can be cooked in the same manner as leeks. The bulbils are wonderful pickled. The underground bulbs have a stronger flavor that tastes better cooked than it does raw.

Cipolline are traditionally served whole in Italy in a sweet-and-sour sauce or they are pickled. These onions are available in farmers' markets or Italian grocers. California-based Frieda's Finest Produce Specialties, Inc. has recently begun to distribute them to select supermarkets. They also marinate well.

Florence long red onions are perfect for a dining-room-table centerpiece, due to their unusual beauty. They are also attractive, and tasty, when sliced and added to salads.

Fresno Sweets, like most red-fleshed onions, should not be cooked because when they are their flavor and texture get watery and they lose their magnificent color.

No More Tears

No matter what the method, you are bound to cry when chopping onions . . . The onion's quality and intensity of flavor, odor, and tear-inducing characteristics depend on the level of sulfuric compounds in the vegetable, which also gives onions their unique flavor. Storage onions have a higher amount of these compounds than fresh onions. Onions gather up through their roots sulfur from the soil. When you peel and slice onions, this chemical is released and can dissolve in the saline solution in your eyes. This produces a very mild form of sulfuric acid, an irritant that causes crying.

How you prepare an onion affects its taste. Chopped raw onion or garlic is stronger-tasting than sliced garlic. That's because the tear-inducing sulfur compounds are activated when cell walls are broken. Know, too, that the heating process of cooking helps destroy the lachrymatory agent and mixture of compounds that taints the breath. The longer bulb onions or garlic are cooked the milder and sweeter they will be in flavor.

- The best way to minimize discomfort when chopping onions is to use a sharp knife and work as carefully but as quickly as possible. It helps to rinse the blade of the knife under cold running water every once in a while while chopping.
- To help reduce tearing when you slice onions, chill them first for 30 minutes. Then cut off the stem, peel off the skin, and cut the onion, waiting to cut off the root end until the last possible moment to help prevent those tears. (The root end has the largest concentration of sulfuric compounds, and it is those compounds that make your eyes tear.)
- Specialty sweet fresh onions are easier to chop; because they are low in the sulfur-containing compounds that make other onions pungent and eye-irritating, you may shed fewer tears when chopping, dicing, or mincing these onions.

Italian sweet red onions are wonderful sliced in salads, sandwiches, and burgers to add color and crunch.

Maui onions are memorable steamed or stir-fried.

Multiplier onions and **potato onions** are both grand pickled or marinated.

Nu-Mex Sweet onions add a special touch when used raw in sandwiches.

Pearl onions are great when parboiled and threaded onto skewers with other kebab ingredients. They are also good in gratins, in a cream sauce, or boiled and combined with peas. You can substitute small boiling onions for them.

Spanish Sweet onions are good raw, sautéed, or even caramelized. A good substitute for specialty sweet fresh onions.

Texas 1015 SuperSweet onions are superb for making onion rings.

Vidalia onions, like most sweet onions, are at their best served raw, but they are equally delicious sautéed, grilled, or baked.

Baby Vidalia onions make a sublime addition to salads or as part of an antipasto platter.

Walla Walla Sweets are terrific served raw in salads.

White onions are great for stewing or sautéeing.

Cooking basics

- Cooking converts the sulfur compounds in onions into sugars, which explains why onions always taste sweeter when cooked.
- To help peel bulb onions, pearl onions, shallots, and garlic more easily, place them in boiling water for 1 minute to loosen their skins, drain, and chill in an ice bath. Then peel off the skin and thin slippery translucent membrane just beneath their skin.
- To keep bulb onions whole and to facilitate even cooking, cut off the stem, trim a very thin slice from the root end and peel off the skins. Then, using the tip of a small paring

knife, cut an "X" in the root end of each onion. This technique works well for pearl onions and shallots also.

- To mellow onions before cooking them, peel and then boil them for 1 minute to remove the bite. Drain well and pat dry with paper towels. To mellow onions before using them raw, slice or chop them, soak them in milk to cover, and refrigerate them, covered, for 30 to 40 minutes. Rinse in a colander under cold running water, drain well, and pat dry with paper towels before using.

- To slice large quantities of bulb onion, shallot, or garlic, use a food processor fitted with a metal blade or slicing disk. Just cut the respective allium to fit the feed tube and process according to desired end result. However, if the allium is destined for a bread product, be sure to drain excess juice off before using, or it might adversely affect the outcome of your baked good. However, do not use a food processor to chop or dice onions, because it tends to turn them to mush.

- To juice an onion, squeeze it just like an orange.

- To remove the smell of onions (or any of the alliums) from your hands or cooking equipment, rub them with lemon juice or vinegar. If the pots are made of aluminum, cast-iron, or carbon-steel, use salt.

- Do not substitute specialty sweet fresh onion for a storage onion because the taste of the fresh will be too delicate. Instead, use the sweet flavor to enhance salads, uncooked relishes, or sauces.

- Follow recipe directions for bulb onions, to see if they are to be cooked until translucent, soft, golden, brown, or crisp. For a mild flavor, cook bulb onions until translucent and tender but not limp. Sauté quickly until golden brown for a more penetrating, sharper taste. Keep a close eye on them as they brown quickly and burn easily. For a mellow, but nutty flavor, brown them slowly, being careful not to scorch them.

- Do not refrigerate leftover peeled, chopped bulb onions, garlic, or shallots overnight because their flavor alters.
- If you have to refrigerate leftover onion, cut off just what you need, don't peel (or chop) the remainder, wrap, refrigerate, and use within 1 day.
- Do not freeze any of the alliums.
- Use stainless steel knives to cut onions; carbon steel will discolor onions.
- Stick a few whole cloves into a whole unpeeled all-purpose yellow onion and place in a stock while it simmers. The onion skin will color the stock slightly, imparting a golden color.
- When in a hurry, substitute frozen chopped onion available at your grocer's freezer. (The commercial freezing process for onions gives results superior to freezing them at home.)

How to Slice or Dice Onions

1. Remove the stem end and peel the skin off.
2. Trim a very thin slice from the root end, but leave the root core intact.
3. Cut the onion in half from stem to root, but leave root core intact.
4. Place each half cut-side down on a work surface. To slice, cut crosswise to desired thickness.
5. To dice, slice horizontally almost to (but not through) the root end, in evenly spaced parallel cuts. The farther apart the cuts are, the larger the dice will be.
6. Make a number of evenly spaced parallel cuts through the top of the onion down to the work surface, but do not cut through the root end. (These cuts will help determine the dice size.)
7. Make crosswise, even, parallel cuts perpendicular to the lengthwise cuts made in Step #6, according to desired dice size (the closer together they are, the smaller the dice).

SCALLIONS

Many people think of scallions as a separate onion species, but they are not. They are simply a collective name given to immature or nonbulbing onion varieties. Scallions have hollow, thin green leaves, white stalks, and are completely edible. They have a gentle, fresh onion flavor that is more assertive than leeks. Many cookbooks specify to use only the white part of the scallion for recipes. I, however, find this very wasteful, because there is a lot of flavor in the green leaves. Unless, of course, you don't want the color of the greens in your recipe, I always recommend using them. Scallions are available year round, peak season being May through July. Since "scallion" seeds (technically onion seeds) can be used to grow spring green onions, sometimes scallions are mistakenly called spring green onions, which as you have read earlier are allowed to develop small bulbs and are only available during the spring.

White Lisbon scallions are grown from seeds of the white Lisbon onion, which was developed especially for use as a scallion. These scallions have tender, juicy green tops, long white stalks, and a mild, sweet flavor with a crisp texture.

Japanese Red Beard scallions are red "green onions," the stalk distinguishable by a red skin. When these onions are grown to size—the bulbs have just begun to swell—they are especially tasty, with a light onion flavor and crunchy texture.

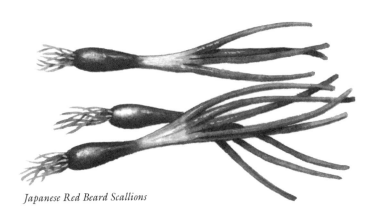

Japanese Red Beard Scallions

The Market and the Cook

When buying scallions, look for those with crisp, dark green leaves, firm white stalks, and no wilt or rot. The root hairs should be white. Do not buy scallions with browned roots or yellow tops; these are signs they have gone beyond their prime.

To store: Loosely wrap scallions in damp paper towels and place in an unsealed plastic bag. If you want to use a perforated plastic vegetable bag, seal it. You can store scallions in the vegetable drawer of the refrigerator for up to three days. If you store them any longer you should peel off and discard the drying outer layers before using them in a recipe.

Recipe match Scallions can be eaten raw, as in crudités when they are served with dip, or in a salad, or cooked briefly, as in a stir-fry, or as a garnish. However you choose to enjoy them, scallions add color, texture, and most important, taste.

Cooking basics Before cooking, rinse scallions under cold running water, cut off the roots, and trim about one-sixteenth of an inch off the root end and any tough leaves. Also remove the thin slippery translucent membrane that covers the white of the stalk. Then cut each scallion in half lengthwise, and cut crosswise as finely as needed.

SHALLOTS

Shallots, also called *eschalots,* are now considered a form of multiplier onion, though they were previously classified in *Allium ascalonicum,* a separate species. Small, elongated bulbs with a tapered end opposite the root end, shallots, unlike many other members of the onion family, never have a bite or are hot; however, they do have a distinct onion flavor, with nutty overtones, and a crisp texture. Wrote the nineteenth-century French gourmet Charles Monselet: "It [the shallot] perfumes without imposing." Shallots do not overpower another ingredient in a dish or disturb the balance of flavors. These bulbs are available year round, peak season being

July through October. Most of the shallots we buy in the United States are from France, supplemented at times by those from South America, and Southeast Asia. Some European strains of shallots are also grown in the United States.

Demi-Long shallots are shiny, copper-skinned, pear-shaped shallots, about walnut size. They have purplish-blue rings of flesh. These shallots are the most common variety found in U.S. supermarkets.

The Market and the Cook

When buying shallots, look for those that are firm and plump, with smooth, dry skin with no spots, bruises, or sprouts. Do not buy withered or dried-out shallots because they will be flavorless. Shallots are best when small, unless, of course, they are specified as "jumbo." Some farmers' markets are now offering baby shallots with the greens still attached. Treat them as you would a spring green onion.

HOW TO SLICE OR DICE SHALLOTS OR GARLIC

1. Separate shallot or garlic into individual cloves.
2. Trim a very thin slice from the stem end, but leave the root end intact.
3. Peel skin away from each clove and lay flat side down on a work surface. To slice, cut crosswise to desired thickness.
4. To dice, slice horizontally almost to (but not through) the root end, in evenly spaced parallel cuts. The farther apart the cuts are, the larger the dice will be.
5. Make a number of evenly spaced parallel cuts through the top of the shallot or garlic down to the work surface, but do not cut through the root end. (These cuts will help determine the dice size.)
6. Make crosswise, even, parallel cuts perpendicular to the lengthwise cuts made in Step #5, according to desired dice size (the closer together they are, the smaller the dice).

To store: Keep shallots like storage onions, in a well-ventilated, cool, dark, dry spot, where they should keep for about three weeks.

Recipe match   Shallots can be eaten raw or cooked. Raw, they are great in salad dressing and vinaigrettes and in cooked form their flavor mellows. Shallots are essential to a number of French sauces, adding just a hint of oniony flavor and slight sweetness.

Cooking basics   Shallots cook quickly, so be careful. They can be blanched, boiled, or roasted right in their skins; the skins slip off easily. Their refined and delicate flavor, though, can be lost in longer-cooking dishes such as stews, unless they are caramelized first. They will hold their shape when cooked, roasted, or caramelized whole.

To peel a shallot: Cut off the tops of the shallots but not the root end. With a knife or your fingers, peel the shallots pulling away the first layer of flesh with the skin that is usually firmly attached to it.

CHAPTER FOUR

Growing Onions

Most of us picture alliums as we see them in the supermarket—scallions lined up in precise bunches; bulb onions piled in heaps or in netted bags. But, lest we forget, onions are plants before they are produce. Growing them from seed or from starter "sets" gives one a new appreciation for these remarkable vegetables. Harold McGee in *On Food and Cooking* says that "at the center of the onion . . . is the beginning of a new life."

That center consists of two stem buds from which the second year's growth arises. Around that core are folded the concentric shells of tissue forming the "rings" of the onion. These shells are really the swollen bases of the previous year's leaves, transformed now into layers of nutrients for the new buds. At the bottom of the bulb is a disk of hardened stem tissue (called a "basal" plate) that holds the scales together. When the bulb is planted or placed in water, roots emerge from this plate. The covering of papery leaves, the onion skin, is called a "tunic"; it protects the bulb from decaying or drying out, while the bulb feeds the leaves and flowers.

Onion bulbs are still alive even when they have been dried through the curing process. Like flower bulbs, they contain within them new plants. When you notice a green shoot sprouting from an onion, that onion has been in your kitchen bin (or supermarket) for too long. This shoot, or sometimes multiple shoots, represents the start of a new plant. These shoots are edible but the layers of onion flesh around them are usually soft and beginning to rot, as they are giving food to this new plant.

Alliums are surprisingly self-sufficient and adaptable. Onions actually produce their own food for the following year and don't even need soil to sprout. In fact, as you have already read, Egyptian top onions practically grow themselves! Although onions grow best without extremes of cold or heat, there is probably no habitable place in the United States where they cannot be grown. All it takes is a little knowledge and care.

You need to know that onion bulbs form in response to both temperature and hours of exposure to sunlight—day-length. Because the onion family must be planted in cool weather, it is considered a cool weather crop. During the very early growing days, green vegetative tips develop—two non-woody parts of the plant that look like small grass blades above ground. Then they die, and are replaced with two new leaves which then grow into four. Later in the growing season wide, waxy, tubular green leaves appear. These green "tops" feed the small bulbs. As the days get warmer, the tops get bushier and growth is concentrated in the expanding bulbs.

Different bulb onion varieties respond to different day-lengths. Those varieties specifically developed for the South won't grow well in the North. You may find yourself harvesting tiny onions when you expected bulbs the size of a fist. Conversely, if you *want* tiny onions, you could plant a variety that needs more daylight than your area provides, thus keeping the bulbs undersized.

If you don't select the right onion seed variety according to your area's latitude, altitude, and temperature, your plants may flower before the bulbs develop, which results in stunted plant growth and onion bulbs smaller than they would be if grown under correct conditions for that seed variety. This occurs because now the plant's food supply is being used to grow the flowers not the bulbs. Early or "short-day" onions require twelve hours of daylight and will mature nicely when planted in the spring in southern areas of the country. "Longer-day" onions need fifteen to sixteen hours of daylight each day, making them ideal for northern areas with long summer days. There are also mid-season onion varieties that do well in mid-latitudes. Seed catalogs or gardening centers can tell you the day-lengths needed for each variety.

Once you know the basics, you can adapt your gardening to your own situation, whether you have a large backyard or small city apartment. Chives, garlic, and scallions grow nicely in containers, as long as they are deep enough for adequate moisture and nutrients. On the other hand, bulb onions, shallots, and leeks are not suitable for indoor container gardens, because they need considerable depth below ground to develop their bulb and root system.

Keep in mind, too, how annual, biennial, and perennial plants differ. Onions and leeks are biennials: They grow and store food in the bulb the first year and flower the second year; then their lifespan is over. Scallions, once picked, must be planted by seed again. For this reason, they are treated as annuals (although technically they are adolescent bulb onions and therefore biennials). Garlic, chives, and shallots are perennials; they come back year after year as long as a portion of the plant is allowed to remain in the ground.

Here is an easy reference guide to planting and harvesting the most common members of the onion family.

CHIVES

Lifespan: Perennial

Companion plants: Tomatoes, carrots, apples, grapes, and roses (*not* peas or beans)

Comments: Chive plants appear in markets, even supermarkets, in late winter. You can grow them in a container on the windowsill.

Outdoor planting: When the soil in your herb garden has warmed up in April, divide the potted clump and plant it outside. Plant early in the spring, in good soil with full sun and good drainage. If you are using seeds, scatter them in a designated area. Water gently—especially at first—if you are planting from seed. In the fall, lift or divide clumps to pot for indoor use in the winter.

Indoor planting: Sow seeds anytime in a six-inch or larger pot filled with good potting soil. Sprinkle 20 or so seeds, then cover lightly with soil. Follow growing instructions as above.

Harvesting: Snip chives off two inches from the bottom with scissors. If picked often, they will remain mild and tender. Every two years, divide the clump and transplant to fresh soil.

GARLIC

Lifespan: Perennial

Companion plants: Roses, potatoes, tomatoes, cucumbers, or cabbage family members (*not* peas or beans)

Comments: Garlic reproduces vegetatively from the cloves of the compound bulb. Each clove forms a new garlic head when planted. Garlic grown in your own garden and properly stored has a fresh pungency unlike the musty odor and bitter flavor too often present in bulbs that have been sitting for too long on a grocery shelf.

To thin the plant rows, the garlic shoots can be clipped when quite young and thin and they still look like scallions, but don't remove the new leaves coming from the bulb centers, because the leaves supply food-energy to the bulbs. Garlic shoots are excellent stir-fried and served as a side dish, simmered in soups, or grilled.

Outdoor planting: Garlic grows best in milder, dry climates. Plant in full sun, in well-drained, loose, somewhat rich soil with good drainage. Northern gardeners should plant sets in the fall so that the root systems can develop before the ground freezes and should mulch with straw during the coldest part of winter. Plants will sprout in the spring. Gardeners in the rest of the country can plant in early spring.

Divide garlic heads into individual cloves; peel them and plant about four inches apart one inch deep in rows that are twelve inches apart. Keep garlic well watered during the first three weeks.

How to Grow Onion Sprouts

Onion sprouts are new to supermarket produce shelves and the stands at farmers' markets. But you can start your own if you just follow these directions. When purchasing seeds to sprout buy them from a reliable source and make sure that they are labeled and recommended for human consumption. Also, do not buy "treated" seeds, and be especially aware of those seeds sold in bulk, which are probably not fit for human consumption. Use only leek seeds that can be used for food purposes. If in doubt, do not use unrecommended seeds. Onion sprouts are delicious when used for sandwiches, salads, and as garnishes.

Use an opaque, not transparent plastic container with a tight-fitting lid to sprout seeds. A friend of mine buys and re-cycles plastic frozen non-dairy whipped topping containers expressly for this purpose.

Step #1 Using the tines of a fork or a metal skewer, punch holds all over the surface of the lid. Spread a layer of seeds on the bottom of the container with just enough cold water to cover. Place the container in a shady, cool place, at room temperature. Let stand for 24 hours, uncovered.

Step #2 Carefully strain and rinse the seeds in a small-meshed sieve, and spread on the bottom of the container. Cover with the lid. Repeat this process twice a day for five days. On the third or fifth day you should see the seed husks split open and tiny shoots appear.

Step #3 After germination, the sprouts grow rapidly as you continue the twice-daily rinsing process. When they are about two inches long and filling the container, they are ready to eat; this usually takes about one week from germination.

When the shoots are up, continue watering every three to five days until you see the stalks emerge. Then begin to cut back on the water, or the bulbs will rot.

Harvesting: Garlic bulbs can take nine months to a year to reach maturity. When the leaves begin to brown, stop watering (the cloves will continue to grow). Garlic is ready for harvesting when the plant tops turn brown and die down. Dig up the heads carefully (but only during a dry period). Cure them outdoors by letting them dry on a screen in the shade. Pull the tops over the bulbs to help protect them further from sunburn for one to three weeks. The skins will dry and become paper-like, readying them for storage. Remember to protect the bulbs from rain during the curing process.

If the heads are to be stored loose (not braided), brush off the soil and cut off the tops (leaving a one- to two-inch stub) and the roots. However, garlic stores best when the tops and roots are not cut off but are braided together to form a garland.

If you are harvesting for immediate use, omit the curing process, promptly refrigerate, and use as soon as possible.

Indoor planting: Separate the cloves of the garlic bulb and discard the smallest. Plant in rich, fertile soil in small, deep pots, one clove to a pot. Stand the pots in a sunny location. As the plant grows, repot as necessary, allowing space for the bulb to develop. If there is enough space in your home, the best way to grow garlic indoors is in a medium-size, cylindrical trash can. Place two or three cloves on a six-inch layer of earth in the bottom of a new, clean trash can, and cover with four inches of soil. Allow plant to grow about four inches tall and then add two more inches of soil. Keep adding soil until it reaches about three inches from top. Water the soil, but don't let it get soggy. Follow outdoor directions for harvesting and curing.

LEEKS

Lifespan: Biennial

Companion plants: Onions, celery, carrots, turnips, beans, and roses

Outdoor planting: Leeks may be started from seeds directly in the garden in spring or late summer, or they may be started in flats indoors and transplanted. Leeks grow slowly, taking 70 to 130 days, depending on the variety. They like fertile soil with good drainage and can tolerate more shade than many vegetables, but will grow even more slowly without full sun. Outdoors, put seeds or plants a quarter inch deep and two inches apart into eight-inch-deep trenches, spaced about eighteen inches apart. The plants should be thinned to stand six inches apart (the thinnings can be eaten like scallions). Throughout the growing season, provide water and fertilizer.

As leeks begin to grow, some gardeners mound soil up around their stem bases, protecting them from air and the blanching effects of the sun. This produces longer white stalks. However, many home gardeners no longer feel the results of blanching are worth the additional work, especially since you can now plant varieties that have been bred to have extra-long white stalks.

Harvesting: Leeks are generally harvested as they are needed, at any stage of growth, and used right away. However, it is best to pick them when the first frost hits. By that time, they will be one to three inches in diameter. Where winters are severe, heavily mulch them, so you can still dig them up throughout the colder months. This step isn't necessary if the temperature rarely drops below 10°F. If the foliage begins to turn yellow, the leek is over-mature, and should be pulled and used right away, and then only to flavor soups or stocks; their texture will be less tender.

BULB ONIONS

Lifespan: Biennial

Companion plants: Lettuce, cabbage family members, beets, carrots, tomatoes, parsnips, roses, and strawberries (*not* asparagus, peas, or beans)

Outdoor planting: Bulb onions are grown from seeds or from young bulbs called "sets." Plant seeds or seedlings one inch deep and four inches apart in rows spaced twelve to twenty-four inches apart. With sets, be sure to plant root end down, pointed tip up. When thinning, pull the largest ones first (they should be one inch across, or less), and then begin pulling every other one from the row. Remember that these thinnings can be eaten as scallions.

As soon as the onions are a few inches tall, add a thick layer of mulch around the plants to help hold back an invasion by weeds. Onions benefit from full sun and rich soil with plenty of organic matter and moisture. Good drainage is also important. If plants start to flower, break off the buds to stimulate greater bulb growth.

As biennials, onions when grown from seed "bulb up" the first year and will flower the second if replanted. When planted from sets, they will usually grow both bulbs and flowers the first year.

Harvesting: Do not harvest bulb onions with the intent to store until their tops die, that is, when the green shoot-like leaves turn yellow, wither, and fall down. Then dig up the plants and let them rest on the soil to dry out for at least a day. Cure them by placing them on a screen outdoors in the shade, with good air circulation, for one to three weeks. Cover them with their tops to shield them from sunburn and be sure to protect them from rain. The skins will become dry and paper-like. This curing process is essential if you want long-lasting onions for storage. When the onions are ready, brush off the soil and clip the tops (leaving a one- to two-inch stub) and cut off the roots at the base. However, for long-term storage, it is best to leave the tops and roots in place, braiding them together to form a garland.

If you are harvesting "fresh onions" to consume immediately (and have decided to omit the curing process), dig up the bulbs, promptly refrigerate them, and use them as soon as possible.

SCALLIONS

Lifespan: Biennial

Companion plants: Lettuce and tomatoes

Comments: Immature onions, scallions are often the first crop in the garden and are picked before the bulbs have a chance to mature.

Outdoor planting: Scallions can be grown from "onion sets" that look like tiny onions (which they are), or planted from seeds and pulled up before the bulb grows too large. Plant them early in the spring, as soon as the ground is workable. Scallions like full sun and somewhat rich, loose soil with good drainage. Sow seeds thinly and keep plants two to three inches apart. Water and weed continuously until harvest.

Indoor planting: One of the best varieties of scallions to grow indoors is the white Lisbon. Use deep containers such as pots and troughs. A somewhat rich soil is an adequate potting medium. Sow seeds at fortnightly intervals from early spring onwards, spreading the seeds as thin as possible. Set the pot on a windowsill that takes full sun and water often to keep soil moist. Germination takes two to three weeks. Once sprouts are visible, thin gradually until plants are three inches apart. As the plants develop, water freely to keep the soil moist, but be careful not to overwater or the roots will rot.

Harvesting: When the tops are six to eight inches tall, pull the scallions right out of the soil.

Indoor harvesting: Scallions can be harvested and eaten at any stage of growth. Those that are left to thicken and grow larger will have a stronger, more oniony flavor.

SHALLOTS

Lifespan: Perennial

Companion plants: Corn and carrots

Outdoor planting: Plant individual bulbs in fall or spring, four inches apart, an inch or two deep, in rows eighteen inches apart. Shallots like full sun and rich, loose soil with good drainage. Keep them watered and weeded.

Harvesting: Shallots are ready to harvest when the leaves start to wither but haven't actually collapsed. Lift the bulbs out of the ground and let them cure outdoors, drying in single layers on screens in the shade for one to three weeks. Pulling the tops over the bulbs keeps them from getting sunburned. They also need protection from rain during the curing process. When the outer skins are dry and paper-like, they are ready for storage.

Do not break the shallot heads into separate bulbs; keep them in clusters. Shallots store best if the tops and roots are left on and are braided together to form a garland. However, if the shallots are to be stored loose, brush off the dirt, clip off the tops (leaving a one- to two-inch stub), and cut off the roots at the base, being careful not to separate the bulbs.

One final note: We may have fond visions of tugging onions from the ground, but it's best to use a garden fork to gently lift garlic, bulb onions, and shallots from the earth. They easily "shatter" in the ground and will crack or bruise if yanked too hard. Scallions and leeks can be pulled carefully from the loose soil, but don't try to tug them if the ground is too hard or frozen. Loosen the soil first, or wait for a thaw. Also kitchen scissors work best for cutting the stems of chives, or snipping the tender green shoots and thinnings from garlic, leek, shallot, and onion plants, which are edible as well. Be sure to cut the tips before they yellow or wither, but spare the new leaves from the heart of the bulb. They herald new life and the gardener's reward—a healthy crop of succulent alliums.

PART TWO

Recipes

Hors D'Oeuvres and Appetizers

Soups and Salads

Entrees

Accompaniments

Desserts and Cakes

Hors D'Oeuvres and Appetizers

Artichoke-Onion Dip

Makes 5 cups

(Can be made 1 day ahead.)

You can alter the hotness of this oniony dip, punctuated with the rich flavor of artichokes and the tang of Mexican tomato salsa, according to the hotness of salsa you use—hot, medium, or mild. I find most people like it best when the salsa is medium-hot.

For best results, make the dip several hours ahead to allow the flavors to develop. Expect a pretty, slight pink cast to it on account of the tomatoes in the salsa. Serve with tortilla chips or crudités.

2 cups light sour cream

1 cup light mayonnaise

1 cup prepared chunky-style tomato salsa

3 cups finely diced red onions or sweet mild onions such as Maui, California Sweet Imperial, Vidalia, Texas 1015 SuperSweet, or Walla Walla

Two 14-ounce cans artichoke bottoms, drained and coarsely chopped

Salt, to taste

3 tablespoons finely chopped fresh chives

1. In a glass bowl combine the sour cream, mayonnaise, tomato salsa, onions, and artichoke bottoms and stir until well blended. Season with salt.

2. Stir in the chives until well blended. Cover and refrigerate 3 hours before serving to allow flavors to blend.

Red Onion Relish Canapés

Makes about ¾ cup relish, or about 2 dozen canapés

(Relish can be made up to 3 days ahead.)

Red onions cook down to form a deep rose-colored, spreadable relish, flavored with the sweetness of honey and the bite of vinegar. Spread on melba toast, or crackers, this makes an ideal topping for canapés for your next cocktail party. If you have any relish left over, try spooning it onto the ends of endive spears—a delicious variation.

1   tablespoon unsalted butter

2   cups finely chopped red onions

2   tablespoons honey

2   tablespoons plus 2 teaspoons red wine vinegar

2   tablespoons plus 2 teaspoons dry red wine

Salt and freshly ground pepper, to taste

Small, square melba toasts, to serve

1. In a heavy nonstick, nonreactive 10-inch skillet melt the butter over medium heat. Add the onions, cover the skillet, and cook the onions about 4 minutes, stirring often, until they soften and release their liquid. Stir in the honey and cook, uncovered, for 5 minutes, stirring often, until the mixture becomes a light golden brown and is lightly caramelized.

2. Pour in the vinegar and wine. Stand back—the mixture will splatter. Bring to a boil, and boil the mixture for 4 minutes, stirring occasionally, or until reduced and almost all the liquid is gone. Season with salt and pepper.

3. Let the mixture cool to room temperature, and serve spread on the melba toast.

Potted Herbed Cheese

Makes about 4 dozen cheese-topped crackers

(Cheese can be made up to 1 day ahead.)

This flavored cheese tastes similar to the popular commercial Boursin, where garlic and onions—in this case, scallions—are accented.

12 ounces low-fat Neufchâtel cream cheese

¾ cup (6 ounces) low-fat small curd cottage cheese

3 cloves garlic, crushed through a garlic press

½ cup very thinly sliced scallions

½ cup minced fresh Italian flat-leaf parsley

Salt, to taste

Crackers, to serve

1. Combine the cream cheese, cottage cheese, garlic, scallions, and parsley in a medium bowl and mix until well blended. Season with salt. Place a small circle of plastic wrap inside the bottom of a medium-sized (or 2 small) clean, new, brightly colored plastic plant pot. Using a rubber spatula, pack the cheese mixture firmly in the pot, smoothing the top. Wrap tightly in plastic wrap and refrigerate until ready to serve. (*Note:* This cheese is best when made 1 day ahead.)

2. To serve, using an indelible marker, label a clean, new plastic plant marker with the recipe title and stick it in the pot. Place the pot in its plant saucer, and fill the saucer with crackers.

Chinese Scallion Pancakes with
Smoked Salmon Tartare

Makes 16 pancakes

1½ cups tartare

Ever since I tasted my first scallion pancakes in a Chinese restaurant, I have wanted to use them in a recipe. Here I have streamlined the lengthy preparation time it usually takes to make them, but you still get spectacular results—bite-size pancakes studded with scallions, with a crisp crust and chewy interior. The lightly combined, intense flavors of smoked salmon tartare as a topping create a trans-ethnic appetizer that is staggeringly good!

Tartare

8 ounces sliced smoked salmon, finely chopped

¼ cup minced white onion

2 tablespoons sesame oil

2 tablespoons drained capers

Pancakes

2 cups unbleached all-purpose white flour, plus more to dust

¾ cup lukewarm water

1 teaspoon salt

1 cup thinly sliced scallions, including green part

4 tablespoons peanut oil

1. To prepare the tartare: Combine the salmon, onion, sesame oil, and capers in a medium bowl and stir until well blended. Cover and reserve at room temperature until ready to use, up to 1 hour ahead.

2. To make the pancakes: Stir together the flour, lukewarm water, and salt in a medium bowl until well blended. (*Note:* The mixture will be very dry, but with kneading will form a dough.)

3. On a lightly floured work surface knead the mixture for 25 turns or until smooth and elastic. (*Note:* The dough should be soft and pliable, not sticky. If it is too dry, add a sprinkling of cold water. If too wet, add a little bit more flour.) Let the dough rest, covered with a damp paper towel, for 20 minutes.

4. On a lightly floured work surface, roll the dough into a 5-inch-long cylinder, and cut into 16 walnut-sized pieces. Using a lightly floured palm, flatten each piece into an even round 2 inches in diameter and $1/4$ inch thick. Pinch each round between your fingers if necessary to help flatten and shape.

5. Dividing the scallions evenly, sprinkle each pancake with an even layer of scallions. Starting with the edge nearest you, roll each pancake up like a jelly roll, while pinching the ends to keep the filling from coming out.

6. Turn each roll seam side up on the work surface. Starting at one end, roll each up so that it resembles a snail, tucking the ends in. Flatten slightly with your palm into a flat 2-inch circle; pinch between your fingers if necessary. Repeat with the remaining dough pieces and keep them covered with damp paper towels.

7. Heat 2 tablespoons of the peanut oil in a heavy 12-inch skillet over high heat until hot but not smoking, and fry the pancakes in two batches of 8 for 2 to 3 minutes on each side (pressing the pancakes flat with a spatula for a few seconds to prevent them from curling), or until a crisp, golden brown crust is formed. Add the remaining oil (the bottom of the skillet should be covered between batches), and heat

until hot but not smoking. Drain the pancakes briefly on paper towels, transfer them to a baking sheet, and keep warm in a preheated 200°F oven.

8. Working quickly, spread each pancake with some salmon tartare and serve at once.

Sea Scallops with Braised Leeks and White Wine

Serves 4

Typically, I do not use cream. However, I could not resist including this recipe, which is based on a very traditional French preparation that includes cream. The trinity of scallops and leeks in cream is one of my favorite taste combinations, and makes a superb hot appetizer.

$1/4$ cup ($1/2$ stick) unsalted butter

10 ounces leeks, tough outer leaves removed, all but 2 inches of dark greens removed, cut in half lengthwise, washed thoroughly, and cut into $1/8$-inch-wide julienne strips

$1/3$ cup dry white wine

$1 1/2$ cups heavy cream, at room temperature

4 shallots, minced

10 ounces sea scallops, muscles removed

Salt and freshly ground white pepper, to taste

1. In a heavy deep 10-inch nonreactive skillet melt the butter over low heat. Stir in the leeks and wine. Cover with a lid or aluminum foil. Cook, stirring often, for 15 to 20 minutes or until the leeks are very tender. Using a slotted spoon, trans-

fer the leeks (leave the juices in the skillet) to a small heat-proof bowl, and cover to keep warm until ready to serve.

2. Add the cream and shallots to the skillet, place over medium heat, and whisk to blend. Bring just to a boil—watch closely, cream has a tendency to boil over—whisking often. Immediately reduce the heat to low and simmer, whisking often, about 15 minutes or until reduced by half. The mixture should coat the back of a spoon.

3. Strain the mixture through a nonreactive fine-meshed strainer set over a bowl, discarding all solid particles. Carefully rinse

ONION GARNISHES

- Make an "onion chrysanthemum" by peeling a medium-sized red onion, leaving the root end intact. Place the onion, root end down, on a cutting board. Cut a shallow "X" on the top of the onion. Using this as a guide, carefully cut the onion into quarters to within $1/4$ inch of the root end. Cut each quarter downwards lengthwise to form thin petals as many times as possible. Place onion in a bowl of ice water and let soak, completely immersed, until the petals open. Drain, blot dry, and use the "chrysanthemum" as a garnish for a cold meat or sandwich platter, or crudité tray.
- Make an "onion bowl" by cutting off the top inch and bottom roots of a peeled large onion so it can stand upright. Cut and scoop out the center, leaving behind $1/4$-inch-thick walls. Use as a bowl in which to serve dips or relishes.
- Make "scallion ruffles" by trimming off and discarding the root ends of a bunch of scallions. Cut off all but four inches of the green tops. Using a sharp, pointed knife, cut the green leaves into thin slivers down to the white stalks. Soak the scallions in a bowl of ice water to cover until the leaves begin to curl. Drain, pat dry, and use as a garnish.

and dry the hot skillet. Return the strained cream mixture to the skillet and place over medium-low heat. Bring to a simmer.

4. Stir the reserved leeks into the cream until well blended. Stir in the scallops and cook for 4 to 5 minutes, stirring often, just until the scallops turn opaque, but are still tender. (*Note:* Be careful not to overcook, or the scallops will be rubbery.) Season with salt and pepper. Serve at once as a hot appetizer.

Shallot-Marsala Confit Tart

Serves 6 to 8 as an appetizer

With its wafer-thin, crisp, flaky crust and rich, jam-like topping, this tart makes an elegant side dish or impressive appetizer. You may also want to serve it as a light entree with a salad.

You can prepare the tart the day of serving, and reheat it just before the guests arrive. Alternatively, make the dough and topping up to two days ahead, so that all you have to do the day of serving is assemble and bake it. However, the tart is best when eaten the day it is baked.

1 ½ cups unbleached all-purpose white flour, plus more to dust

1 teaspoon salt

½ cup (1 stick) unsalted butter or margarine, cut into 8 pieces and chilled

1 large egg yolk lightly whisked with 2 tablespoons cold water

3 to 4 tablespoons ice water

1 cup Shallot-Marsala *Confit* (recipe follows)

1. Sift together the flour and salt in a medium bowl. Using a pastry blender or fork, cut in the chilled butter a few pieces

at a time, until mixture resembles coarse crumbs. Stir in the egg yolk with the 2 tablespoons cold water until well blended. Then stir in the ice water a tablespoon at a time, as needed to allow the dough to form but not become sticky. Form into a flat disk, wrap in waxed paper, and chill for 30 minutes. (Dough can be made up to 2 days ahead.)

2. Preheat the oven to 425°F.

3. On a lightly floured work surface roll out the dough into a rectangle $1/8$ inch thick. Line an ungreased 13 by 9 by 2-inch baking dish with the dough, allowing $1/2$ inch of the dough to come up all 4 sides to form a raised edge. Trim the edges neatly.

4. Spread the shallot-Marsala *confit* in an even layer over the dough and smooth the surface. Prick the surface of the tart (through the filling) all over with a fork (to keep the crust flat while baking).

5. Bake in the middle third of the oven for 15 to 20 minutes or until the edges of the crust are crisp and a delicate brown. (*Note:* Watch the tart carefully; if it starts to bubble and the crust begins to lift off the baking dish, use a fork to prick the surface again all over.)

6. Let stand for 10 minutes. With a serrated knife, cut into slices and serve hot, or at room temperature. Serves 8 as an appetizer, or 6 as a side dish.

Shallot-Marsala Confit

Makes 1 cup

(Can be made up to 3 days ahead.)

This intensely flavored dish makes all the effort involved in peeling shallots worthwhile, especially since you can store the *confit* in the refrigerator for up to three days. And the flavor of shallots marries perfectly with Marsala, a fortified Italian dessert wine with a whisper of toasted nuts in the bouquet. In fact, shallot-Marsala *confit* is the pinnacle of shallot flavor. The natural sugar of this onion relative caramelizes, becoming the base for the *confit*.

Use this as you would any condiment, or toss it with hot pasta for a sensational combination. It is also wonderful spread on grilled (or broiled) fish fillets or chicken breasts hot off the fire. For a gourmet touch to brunch the day after Easter dinner, smear hot split biscuits with the *confit*, then tuck leftover slices of Easter ham in between.

Use fresh thyme if available, because the texture of the fresh leaves is unobtrusive, whereas dried thyme can have a "woody," noticeable presence.

24 ounces shallots, unpeeled

1/4 cup (1/2 stick) unsalted butter (*Note:* Do not substitute margarine because it tends to add a fishy flavor.)

1 teaspoon salt

1 teaspoon freshly ground pepper

2 tablespoons sugar

1 tablespoon finely chopped fresh thyme or 1 teaspoon dried, crumbled

1/2 cup dry Marsala

1. Bring a heavy 4-quart saucepan of water to a boil over medium heat. Add the shallots, bring to a second boil, and boil for 1 minute. Drain at once in a colander and plunge the shallots into an "ice bath" (a bowl of ice water). Using a knife, peel, trim the ends, and thinly slice the shallots.

2. Melt the butter in a heavy 10-inch skillet over medium heat. Add the shallots, salt, and pepper and cook, covered with a lid or foil, stirring often, for 10 minutes.

3. Stir in the sugar, thyme, and Marsala and cook, uncovered, stirring frequently, for 8 to 10 minutes or until the shallots are a deep golden brown and beginning to fall apart, forming a thick puree. (This recipe can be prepared up to 3 days ahead. Let cool; cover and refrigerate.)

Grilled Leeks Sesame

Serves 4

This simple dish abounds with onion flavor. For the sake of presentation and portion size, choose smaller leeks to serve as an appetizer, medium-size leeks as a side dish.

4 medium leeks (about 2 pounds), tough outer leaves removed, 4 inches of the greens removed, cut in half lengthwise to within 1/2 inch of trimmed root end, leaving leeks whole, and washed thoroughly (*Note:* Choose leeks as similar in size as possible.)

1 teaspoon sesame oil, to brush

2 tablespoons sesame seeds, to garnish

Salt and freshly ground pepper, to taste

1. In a large pot bring 3 quarts lightly salted water to boil over high heat. Using butcher's twine, tie the leeks together and place in the pot. Return the water to a boil, and boil the leeks for 6 to 8 minutes (4 to 6 minutes for small leeks), or until tender when tested with a fork. Drain and rinse under cold running water. Untie the leeks and pat dry with paper towels. (Recipe can be made up to this point 1 day ahead. Wrap leeks tightly in plastic wrap and refrigerate.)

2. Preheat the grill and brush the leeks all over with sesame oil. Grill the leeks over medium-high heat for 7 to 9 minutes (4 to 7 minutes for small leeks), turning frequently, until they are very tender when pierced with a fork and have grill marks all over.

3. While the leeks are grilling, wrap the sesame seeds in aluminum foil and place on the grill rack near the edge. Toast for 3 to 4 minutes or until the sesame seeds are lightly browned. Keep the leeks warm in a low-temperature oven until ready to serve. Season the leeks with salt and pepper, sprinkle with sesame seeds to garnish, and serve.

Spicy Onion Fritters with Roasted Tomato Dipping Sauce

Serves 6

(Sauce can be made up to 2 days ahead.)

Crunchy on the outside and soft and pillowy within, these fritters make a great finger food to serve before dinner as an appetizer, but they also make a wonderful light meal for four when served with a salad. The roasted onion in the dipping sauce not only adds zing to the dish as a whole, but intensifies the onion flavor in the fritters. Though onion fritters in India are usually spiced with green chilies, I have replaced them with a Thai-style red curry paste, also hot, for a spicy and fragrant trans-ethnic dish.

Sauce (Makes 1 cup)

1   medium-size ripe tomato

2   tablespoons olive oil, to brush

1   medium red onion, cut into ¼-inch-thick slices and rings separated

Salt and freshly ground pepper, to taste

Fritters

1 cup toasted garbanzo bean (chick-pea) flour (available at health food stores)

2 teaspoons peanut oil

$^3/_4$ teaspoon ground cumin

1 teaspoon salt

2 teaspoons Thai-style red curry paste (available from Williams-Sonoma: WILLIAMS-SONOMA, Mail-Order Department, P.O. Box 7456, San Francisco, CA 94120-7456, Telephone: (415) 421-4242 (or 1-800-541-2233), shops and mail order, or from Asian markets)

$^1/_2$ cup warm water (90–100°F)

2 cups finely chopped white onions (about 2 medium)

$2^1/_2$ quarts peanut oil

1. Preheat the oven to 450°F.

2. To make the sauce: Core the tomato, and place it in a medium shallow baking dish. Rub the entire surface of the tomato with some of the olive oil. Surround the tomato with the onion rings and toss with the remaining olive oil. Bake in the middle third of the oven for 20 minutes or until the tomato is very soft and the skin begins to blister. Remove the dish from the oven and let the tomato and onion rings cool to room temperature. Peel the skin off the tomato and discard.

3. Transfer the tomato and onion to the bowl of a food processor fitted with a metal blade and process for about 2 minutes or until pureed. Season with salt and pepper. Transfer to a medium glass bowl, cover, and refrigerate until ready to serve. (Sauce can be made up to 2 days ahead.)

4. To prepare the fritters: Combine the flour and the 2 teaspoons peanut oil in a large bowl. Pick up some of the flour and oil and rub between your palms; continue this

process until the entire batch of flour in the bowl is evenly coated with oil, and no lumps remain. (*Note:* This rubbing technique helps make for a crispy crust.) Stir in the cumin, salt, and curry paste until well blended. Using an electric mixer on medium-high speed, add the warm water in a thin stream and continue to beat constantly for 5 minutes until mixture becomes smooth, lighter in texture, and slightly lighter in color.

5. Cover the bowl with plastic wrap and let rest in a warm, draft-free place for 30 minutes. Stir in the onions until well blended.

6. Heat the oil in a heavy 6-quart pot (the oil should reach a depth of 2 inches) over medium-high heat until it reads 375°F on a deep-fry thermometer. To test, drop a little batter into the oil. If it sinks and then rises to the surface, the oil is hot enough.

7. When the oil is ready, drop the batter into the oil in 2-tablespoon amounts, making 6 fritters at a time. Do not crowd the pot—the fritters should not touch each other. (*Note:* Be careful and wear flameproof mitts when frying.) Fry the fritters, turning often, for 3 to 6 minutes per batch, or until their surface is crisp and golden brown. (*Note:* When the fritters are added, the temperature of the oil will automatically drop; keep the temperature at a constant 375°F by regulating the burner heat between medium-high and medium-low.)

8. Using a slotted metal spoon, transfer the fritters to a paper-towel-lined platter to drain briefly, then to a baking sheet to keep warm in a low-temperature preheated oven. Repeat the process with the remaining ingredients, skimming the surface of the oil in between batches to keep it clean. Serve the fritters at once accompanied by a bowl of the dipping sauce.

Irma Rhode's Onion Sandwiches

Makes 1 dozen or more sandwiches

"I can easily make a whole meal of onion sandwiches, for to me they are one of the greatest treats I know. . . . " wrote James Beard, the famous chef and food author, in his book *Beard on Food*.

When I am feeling hungry, I add lettuce, tomato, and bacon to this for a spunky, very substantial BLT. And while James Beard made his own mayonnaise, I have suggested using store-bought. The following recipe was contributed to the *James Beard Celebration Cookbook* by Craig Claiborne.

24 thin slices firm-textured bread, such as challah or brioche

6 tablespoons mayonnaise

12 wafer-thin onion slices

Salt, to taste

Freshly ground black pepper, to taste

1 cup finely chopped parsley

1. Using a 1³⁄₄-inch cookie cutter, cut out rounds from the centers of the bread slices (the number may vary from 1 to 3, depending on the size of the cookie cutter and the size of the bread slices).

2. With a small spatula spread mayonnaise on each of the 24 bread rounds. The diameter of the onion slices should approximate that of the bread rounds. Sprinkle each with salt and pepper. Place one onion slice on 12 of the rounds. Cover with a bread round, mayonnaise side down.

3. Using the spatula, smear the outside rim of the sandwich with mayonnaise, coating fairly liberally. Roll the rim of each sandwich in the parsley to coat it generously. Continue until all the sandwiches are coated, adding more ingredients as necessary. Cover and chill for 1 hour.

Soups and Salads

Miso Shiru
(Japanese Bean Curd Soup)

Serves 4, 2 cups each

I have always felt that *miso* soup, a very nutritious national dish of Japan, really shows off the crisp, flavorful, and decorative qualities of the scallion. Scallions are sprinkled into the clear soup as garnish but are truly essential to the soup as a whole.

I like to make this amber-colored, delicately flavored soup with a *shiitake* mushroom (Japanese forest mushroom) broth base, along with clam juice. Use only dried *shiitake* mushrooms for the most flavorful essence.

In Japan, the season dictates what is added to this soup. For example, snow peas might be included in the spring, while potato and green beans could be added in the fall.

Two 14½-ounce cans low-sodium chicken broth

Two 8-ounce bottles all-natural clam juice

2 cups boiling water

1¾ ounces dried *shiitake* mushrooms (available at Oriental markets, gourmet shops, or health food stores)

2 tablespoons *mirin* (Japanese sweet cooking wine, available at most Oriental markets and gourmet shops)

¼ cup *mugi miso* (barley *miso,* available at health food stores or Oriental markets), blended with ½ cup hot water until the *miso* has dissolved

8 ounces very firm or firm tofu (bean curd, available at supermarkets), drained and cut into ½-inch cubes

2 tablespoons teriyaki sauce (Japanese soy-based sauce)

2 tablespoons soy sauce or more, to taste

½ cup thinly sliced scallions, including greens, cut on the diagonal

Notes: Mirin, a traditional Japanese seasoning and sweetening agent, is made from *sake* (Japanese rice wine), sweet rice, and rice malt.

There are several types of *miso* (fermented soybean paste). For this recipe, I have called for *mugi miso,* which has barley added. There is also a very savory, richly flavored, mellow type called "red *miso.*" Store all *miso* tightly wrapped in the refrigerator.

1. Combine the chicken broth, clam juice, and the 2 cups boiling water in a 5-quart pot. Remove from the heat and stir in the dried mushrooms. Cover with a lid slightly smaller than the pot so that the lid pushes down the mushrooms and they are submerged. Let stand at room temperature for 30 minutes to reconstitute the mushrooms. Once they are soft, using a slotted spoon, remove the mushrooms, reserving the broth. Remove and discard the stems and cut the caps into $\frac{1}{4}$-inch-wide slices; reserve.

2. Place the pot with the reserved broth mixture over low heat and bring to a simmer. Stir in the reserved *shiitake* mushrooms and *mirin.* Stir in the *miso*-water mixture until well blended, add the tofu cubes, and simmer for 5 minutes until hot. (*Note:* Do not let boil, or the digestion-aiding enzymes of the *miso* will be destroyed.) Stir in the teriyaki sauce and soy sauce, and adjust the seasonings to taste.

3. Ladle the soup into 4 bowls, sprinkle evenly with the scallions, and serve.

No-Cream Leek and Potato Soup

Serves 4, about 3 cups each

Serves 6, about 2 cups each

Based on the flavor pairings of classic vichyssoise, but made without cream and served hot, this vegetarian soup has a lovely golden color and an unpretentious homemade appearance—a great soup-in-a-mug: Some of the potatoes fall apart to thicken the soup, while others stay whole for texture, and the leeks and other vegetables add a natural sweetness.

Wait to peel and cut the potatoes until just before using them to avoid any discoloration. If you want, add the peels from the potatoes for more body and flavor, but keep in mind that this will give the soup a very rustic appearance.

3 tablespoons olive or canola oil

1 large Spanish Sweet onion or 2 medium white onions, coarsely chopped

3 carrots, thinly sliced

3 ribs celery, thinly sliced

1½ pounds leeks, tough outer leaves removed, all but 2 inches of the greens removed, cut in half lengthwise, washed thoroughly, and thinly sliced

6 medium baking potatoes (about 3¾ pounds), peeled and cut into ½-inch dice

Three 14½-ounce cans vegetable broth (available at supermarkets)

1 bay leaf, broken in half

¼ cup minced fresh chives, to garnish

⅛ cup minced fresh parsley, to serve

Salt and freshly ground pepper, to taste

1. Heat the oil in a heavy 6-quart pot over medium heat. Add the onion, carrots, celery, and leeks and cook about 10 min-

utes, stirring frequently, or until the onion, celery, and leeks are tender and the carrots crisp-tender.

2. Stir in the potatoes, vegetable broth, and bay leaf, and bring to a boil.

3. Reduce the heat to low and simmer, stirring occasionally, for 30 to 40 minutes, or until the vegetables are very soft and the potatoes are beginning to fall apart. Remove and discard the bay leaf halves.

4. Just before serving, stir in the chives and parsley. Season with salt and pepper and serve hot.

Classic French Onion Soup

Serves 6, 1½ to 2 cups each

(Soup can be made up to 3 days in advance through Step #2; return to simmer before proceeding.)

On a cold winter's evening, there is nothing more wonderful than sitting down to a glass of robust red wine and a small balloon-shaped earthenware pot of steaming onion soup graced with melted cheese. The soup will likely stir memories of your last visit to France.

Generally a sweeter onion is used to make this soup, but I prefer an all-purpose onion, which maintains its characteristic flavor even after long periods of cooking. Typically, beef stock is called for, but I suggest using chicken stock; its lighter taste allows the flavor of the onions to come forth and is complemented by the Madeira, which replaces the usual splash of brandy. To make up for the reduced sweetness, I simply add a little sugar. However, the secret of this soup resides in the slow cooking of the onions, which releases their rich flavor and natural sugar.

By all means, use a food processor to slice the onions. Simply cut them into chunks that will fit through the feed tube, then process with a medium slicing disk.

$\frac{1}{2}$ cup (1 stick) unsalted butter

2   pounds all-purpose yellow onions, thinly sliced

2   tablespoons sugar

$\frac{1}{4}$ cup all-purpose flour

6   cups rich homemade chicken stock or canned low-sodium chicken broth

$\frac{1}{2}$ cup dry sherry

3   tablespoons Madeira

Salt and freshly ground pepper, to taste

Twelve 1-inch-thick slices of French baguette

2   tablespoons olive oil

1 clove garlic, halved lengthwise

2   cups shredded French Gruyère cheese (Comté) or Swiss Gruyère cheese (a 6-ounce rindless piece)

1.   Melt the butter in a heavy 6-quart pot over medium-low heat. Add the onions and cover. Cook slowly, stirring occasionally, for 10 minutes. Reduce the heat to low, stir in the sugar, and continue to cook for 30 minutes, uncovered, stirring frequently, or until the onions are beginning to fall apart and are straw-colored, making sure to scrape the bottom of the pot with the spoon to keep the contents from burning. (*Note:* Depending on the amount of sugar in the onions you use, the onions may turn golden-brown at this step.) Sprinkle in the flour and stir for 30 seconds.

2.   Stir in the stock, sherry, and Madeira: Stand back—the contents will splatter. Cover and simmer, stirring occasionally, for 10 minutes. And season to taste with salt and pepper.

3.   Preheat the oven to 400°F.

4.   Using a pastry brush, coat both sides of the bread slices lightly with the olive oil. Arrange the bread slices in a single layer on a baking sheet and bake in the top third of the

oven for 5 minutes per side or until completely dry and the edges are lightly golden brown. When cool enough to handle, rub both sides of each bread slice with the halved clove of garlic and set aside.

5. Set the broiler rack about 6 inches from the heat source, and preheat the broiler.

6. To serve, ladle the soup into 6 earthenware French onion soup pots or ovenproof soup bowls with 2-cup capacity each. Sprinkle with half of the cheese. Top each with 2 bread slices, pressing them into the soup so their edges will not burn. Sprinkle with the remaining cheese, and place the pots under the broiler. Broil for 1 to 2 minutes or just until the cheese melts, bubbles, and begins to brown. Serve at once.

Wintertime Double-Onion Soup with Cottage Cheese–Scallion Dumplings

Serves 4, about 2 cups with 4 dumplings each

Close your eyes and picture enjoying this soup with its heaven-sent, airy, fluffy dumplings bobbing on a rich brown surface on a January day in a bitterly cold part of the world, where only something warm and soothing at dinnertime will suffice.

I refer to this soup as "double-onion" because it contains two types of onions: scallions in the dumplings and bulb onions in the soup base. The flavor imparted from ingredients like the dumplings, tomato paste, sage, and bay leaves makes this soup entirely different from the Classic French Onion Soup on page 86.

As just mentioned, an important ingredient in this preparation is bay leaves, one of my favorite seasonings. Unfortunately, most people store bay leaves far too long, thinking they keep better than other herbs and spices. After three months in the spice rack, however, the leaves start to lose their potency. So, before adding them to this soup, please make sure they are fresh.

And here's another tip: The steaming of the dumplings in the soup adds thickness to the broth. Should you decide to omit the dumplings—but don't, they are fabulous!—increase the amount of flour in the soup base by one more tablespoon.

Dumplings

1¾ cups unbleached all-purpose white flour

1 tablespoon double-acting baking powder

½ teaspoon salt

¾ cup milk (2% milk, if desired)

½ cup low-fat small curd cottage cheese

½ cup thinly sliced scallions, including green part

Soup

3 tablespoons unsalted butter

2 pounds all-purpose yellow onions, thinly sliced

2 tablespoons all-purpose flour

6 cups canned low-sodium beef broth

3 cups canned low-sodium vegetable broth (available at supermarkets)

3 tablespoons tomato paste

¼ cup brandy

2 bay leaves, each broken in half

2 teaspoons minced fresh sage or 1 teaspoon ground dried sage

½ teaspoon salt

½ teaspoon freshly ground pepper

1. To prepare the dumplings: Combine the flour, baking powder, and salt in a small bowl and stir until well blended. Add the milk, cottage cheese, and scallions, and stir until mixture forms a sticky dough. Cover and refrigerate until ready to use.

2. To make the soup: In a heavy 6-quart pot melt the butter over low heat and stir in the onions. Cook, stirring often, for 30 to 35 minutes or until the onions are soft and straw-colored. (*Note:* Watch the onions carefully to be sure that they do not burn.)

3. Sprinkle the flour over the onions and cook, stirring, for 3 minutes. Raise the heat to medium, stir in both broths, the tomato paste, brandy, bay leaves, sage, salt, and pepper, and bring to a boil, stirring occasionally. Reduce the heat to low and cook for 25 minutes, stirring occasionally. Remove and discard the bay leaf halves.

4. To cook the dumplings: One at a time, measure 1 heaping rounded tablespoonful of dumpling batter and drop it into the pot. (You should have 16 irregularly shaped dumplings.) In about 1 minute, the dumplings will rise, and cover the entire surface of the pot. Cover tightly and let the dumplings simmer undisturbed (do not lift the lid) for 15 to 20 minutes or until a toothpick inserted in the center of a dumpling comes out clean. (*Note:* Do not let the soup reach a temperature higher than a simmer or the dumplings won't be light in texture.)

5. To serve, using a slotted spoon, divide the dumplings among 4 soup bowls, ladle the soup around them, and serve hot.

Emerald Soup with Walla Walla–Mint Butter

Serves 4, 2 cups each

I named this cream of broccoli and watercress soup "emerald soup" because of its lovely color. Made with half-and-half instead of heavy cream, it is rich in vegetal flavor. The crowning touch is the onion-mint butter, which can be made one day ahead but no earlier because both the flavor and texture of the onion will change.

Butter

$\frac{1}{2}$ cup (1 stick) unsalted butter, at room temperature

$\frac{1}{2}$ cup minced Walla Walla onion or other sweet mild onion such as Maui, California Sweet Imperial, Vidalia, or Texas 1015 SuperSweet

$\frac{1}{4}$ cup finely chopped fresh mint

Soup

$2\frac{1}{2}$ pounds broccoli, with stems

6 tablespoons unsalted butter

Two 8-ounce bunches watercress, with stems, finely chopped

4 cups water

2 cups half-and-half, at room temperature

Salt and freshly ground pepper, to taste

1. To make the butter: In a small bowl beat the butter until soft. Fold in the onion and fresh mint until well blended.

2. Transfer the butter to a rectangular sheet of waxed paper and form it into a cylindrical shape about 5 inches long. Fold the waxed paper just over the butter. Place a long pencil against the paper-covered cylinder. Push the pencil against the butter, while holding the edges of the waxed paper in

place. (This will help form an even cylinder and remove all air bubbles.) Gently roll up the log of butter and tightly twist the ends closed, being careful not to disturb the form. Wrap in 2 layers of aluminum foil and chill until firm enough to slice. Flavored butter can be made up to this point 1 day ahead.

3. To make the soup: Cut off the broccoli florets, cut them into bite-size pieces, and reserve. Using a vegetable peeler, peel the broccoli stems (discard the peels) and finely chop the stems.

4. Melt the butter in a 5-quart nonreactive saucepan over medium heat. Add the watercress, and cook, stirring, about 4 minutes or until soft. Add the broccoli stems and reserved florets with the 4 cups water. Bring to a boil, then cover. Reduce the heat to medium-low and cook, stirring occasionally, 12 to 15 minutes, until broccoli is *very* tender and beginning to fall apart. Let cool until soup can be easily handled.

5. Transfer the vegetables and cooking liquid to a blender and blend in three batches on high, about 3 minutes per batch, or until very smooth.

6. Return the pureed soup to the nonreactive saucepan. Place the saucepan over medium heat and bring to a simmer, stirring.

7. Stir the half-and-half into a small bowl with ½ cup of the hot soup, then stir this back into the pot until well blended. Cook, stirring, for 4 minutes or until heated through; do not let boil. (*Note:* If soup is thicker than desired, thin out with a little warm water.) Season with salt and pepper.

8. To serve, unwrap the butter, cut the log in half crosswise, and cut one half into 8 slices. (You will need only 4 slices, so save the remainder for another use.) Divide the soup among 4 shallow soup bowls and top each with a slice of the butter. When the butter melts, guests can stir it into the soup.

Summertime Tomato and Scallion Aspic

Serves 4

There is nothing so refreshing as cooling tomato aspic on a hot summer day. And because canned tomatoes are available year round, you can make this delicious dish anytime you please. For added flavor and color, the recipe below uses chopped scallions to offset the smooth texture of the aspic. Not surprisingly, aspics are a Southern tradition. They are usually accompanied by mayonnaise, but I like mine served as is, on a lettuce-lined plate, as a salad course. It makes a striking accompaniment to a seafood entree like Shrimp Creole.

If you have any aspic left over, use it to make this tasty sandwich: Spread the aspic on a slice of bread. Spread mustard on the other bread slice, top with several whole fresh basil leaves and some sliced Swiss cheese; then assemble and enjoy.

Olive oil, to grease ramekins

One 28-ounce can whole tomatoes

2 tablespoons minced fresh tarragon

2 envelopes unflavored powdered gelatin

$1/4$ cup cold water

$1/4$ cup very thinly sliced scallions

Salt and freshly ground pepper, to taste

Tabasco sauce, to taste

Lettuce leaves, to serve

1. Lightly grease the inside and the rim of 4 ramekins, each with a $3/4$- to 1-cup capacity, with olive oil.

2. Add the tomatoes and their juice to the bowl of a food processor fitted with a metal blade. Process for 1 minute or until the tomatoes are pureed. Transfer the tomatoes with 1 tablespoon of the tarragon to a nonreactive 3-quart saucepan and place over medium heat. Bring to a boil, stirring

occasionally. Reduce the heat to low and simmer for 20 minutes, stirring occasionally.

3. Carefully strain the tomato mixture through a fine-mesh strainer into a bowl, pressing on the contents with the back of a wooden spoon to help force them through. Discard all solid particles, reserving the warm juice.

4. Soften the gelatin in the cold water. Stir the gelatin into the reserved warm juice until dissolved. Set the bowl over a larger bowl of ice water and stir occasionally until the aspic begins to thicken, about 10 minutes. Stir in the remaining 1 tablespoon tarragon and the scallions, and adjust the seasoning with salt, pepper, and Tabasco sauce, to taste.

5. Pour into the prepared ramekins, cover, and chill for 3 hours or until set. Turn out onto lettuce-lined salad plates and serve chilled.

Fresh Fennel, Orange, and Red Onion Salad with Mint Dressing

Serves 4 to 6

This zesty, colorful salad is rousing in its combination of refreshing ingredients like juicy oranges and licorice-flavored fennel. I like to use blood oranges, but they are only available in the United States late June through early July, and even then may be difficult to find except in gourmet produce markets or better supermarkets. Navel oranges also work nicely and enable you to make the salad more frequently. Whether you are using blood or navel oranges, there should be twice as many orange slices as onions.

Fresh fennel should be trimmed of its tough exterior strings before cooking or eating. When trimming (see instructions below), make sure to set aside some of the feathery leaves as they make a flavorful garnish on the salad.

6 medium blood oranges or 3 medium navel oranges, peeled, being careful to remove all the pith (spongy outer white membrane), and sliced crosswise into $\frac{1}{4}$-inch-thick rounds

1 small red onion, cut to fit a food processor feed tube and cut with a medium slicing disk; rings separated

1 medium bulb fresh fennel (about 1 pound), trimmed (how-to procedure follows) and finely chopped, reserving feathery leaves for the dressing and garnish, if desired

3 tablespoons extra-virgin olive oil

1 tablespoon white wine vinegar

$\frac{1}{4}$ cup finely chopped fresh mint

2 teaspoons coarse-grain mustard

1 teaspoon sugar

$\frac{1}{2}$ teaspoon salt

$\frac{1}{4}$ teaspoon freshly ground pepper

1 tablespoon finely minced fresh fennel leaves

To Trim Fennel

Cut off the upper stalks. Make about a $\frac{1}{4}$-inch cut into and around the edge of each stalk top (but not all the way through), then one by one, holding these partially cut pieces away from you, pull them toward the fennel bulb base, pulling the outer strings with them and discarding them. Trim off the woody end of the bulb base. Core and proceed to cut according to recipe directions.

---

1. Arrange the orange slices in a wide shallow platter, overlapping them. Top with a layer of the onion rings and sprinkle them with the chopped fennel.

2. Combine the olive oil, vinegar, mint, mustard, sugar, salt, pepper, and fennel leaves in a small bowl and whisk to combine. Drizzle the dressing over the salad and tightly cover with plastic wrap.

3. Let stand at room temperature for at least 3 hours before serving or up to 6. Every so often, spoon the juices that have collected in the platter over the salad and re-cover.

4. To serve, arrange the salad on individual salad plates and drizzle with the dressing.

Jennifer Brennan's Papaya and Shrimp Salad
(Som Tam)

Serves 6 to 8

This recipe is from Jennifer Brennan's *The Original Thai Cookbook*. In Thailand, *som tam* is made with green (unripe) papaya, which is not available in the United States; but ripe, firm papaya makes a very attractive and flavorful alternative.

1 small head iceberg lettuce, separated into leaves

½ small head green cabbage, finely shredded

2 medium papayas, peeled, seeded, and thinly sliced

2 firm but ripe, medium tomatoes, sliced

8 ounces cooked Bay shrimp, peeled and deveined

2 tablespoons shelled peanuts, coarsely crushed

2 fresh green serrano chiles, seeded (how-to procedure follows) and cut into very thin slivers (available at supermarkets or greengrocers)

Juice of 3 limes

2 tablespoons fish sauce (*nam pla*) available at Oriental markets)

2 tablespoons palm sugar (available at Oriental markets)

2 scallions, including greens, finely chopped

1. Arrange the lettuce leaves on a platter. In a bowl combine the shredded cabbage, papaya slices, and tomatoes, reserving a few tomato slices for garnish. Place mixture on the bed of lettuce and sprinkle with the shrimp and peanuts. Garnish with the reserved tomato slices and the chiles.

2. In a small bowl mix together the lime juice, fish sauce, palm sugar, and scallions until the sugar has dissolved. Pour dressing over the salad. Cover and refrigerate until ready to serve.

HOW TO HANDLE AND PREPARE FRESH CHILE PEPPERS

Wear rubber gloves when handling fresh chile peppers, and never touch your face—eyes or nose—because the oil from the chiles can act as an irritant to your skin and mucous membranes. After handling the chiles, wash your hands, the cutting board, and knife with warm soapy water.

Before cutting the chile pepper, rinse it and pull the stem out under cold running water. The heat of the chile (an alkaloid called capsaicin) is more concentrated in the seeds and ribs than in its meat, so to prepare the chiles for cooking, cut the pod in half lengthwise and brush out and discard the seeds. Using a sharp paring knife, cut out the fleshy ribs and discard. The chile can now be used or it can be soaked briefly in lightly salted cold water to help reduce some of the heat.

[*Note:* If you do get chile oil on your skin and you feel a burning sensation, apply a paste of baking soda and cold water (a ratio of 2:1) to the affected area and allow to dry, then wipe off. If you get some oil in your eyes, rinse them with cold water.]

Salmon Cakes with Garlic Tartar Sauce on Watercress

Makes 8 servings of 2 cakes each

These fish cakes make an exquisite departure from the traditional crab-based ones. Typically less expensive than crab, salmon adds a touch of elegance and refinement worth much more than its cost.

To save time, broil the salmon before flaking it, or use the marvelous (but often overlooked) cans of pink or red salmon. On a strict diet? Omit the tartar sauce and serve just the cakes with fresh lemon wedges to squeeze at the table. But be warned! Tartar sauce is very popular, and when spiked with garlic it is even more of a crowd pleaser—irresistible to all garlic lovers. Your guests may crave it, and will probably ask for more. For that reason, I created a recipe that makes extra sauce, so you can pass it at the table.

Tartar Sauce (Makes about 2¼ cups)

3/4 cup light mayonnaise

3/4 cup light sour cream

3 tablespoons Dijon-style mustard

3 tablespoons sweet pickle relish

3 tablespoons drained capers, finely chopped

5 medium cloves garlic, crushed through a garlic press

Salmon Cakes

1/2 cup minced celery

1/2 cup very thinly sliced scallions, including the greens

1 cup dry unseasoned bread crumbs

1 tablespoon finely chopped fresh dill or 1 teaspoon dried, crumbled

2 teaspoons Dijon-style mustard

$^1/_2$ teaspoon salt

1 teaspoon freshly ground pepper

3 dashes Tabasco sauce

$^1/_8$ teaspoon ground nutmeg

2 large egg whites

2 salmon steaks, about $^1/_2$ pound each, cooked, cooled, skin and bones discarded, and flaked into medium-sized pieces; or substitute three 6$^1/_2$-ounce cans pink (or red) skinless, boneless chunk salmon, bones and gray parts removed and discarded

3 tablespoons canola or vegetable oil, plus more if needed, to fry

2 bunches watercress, trimmed, washed well, and dried, to line salad plates

1. To make the tartar sauce: Combine the mayonnaise, sour cream, mustard, relish, capers, and garlic in a medium nonreactive bowl and stir until well blended. (*Note:* This sauce is best made 1 day ahead to allow the flavors to blend.) Cover and refrigerate until serving. Serve chilled.

2. To prepare the salmon cakes: Combine the celery, scallions, bread crumbs, dill, mustard, salt, pepper, Tabasco sauce, and nutmeg, and stir until well blended. Stir in the egg whites briefly, just until mixture is moistened, then fold in the flaked salmon until well blended. The mixture should be moist enough to stick together. (*Note:* If mixture is too moist to work with, refrigerate it for 15 minutes before forming into patties.)

3. Using your hands, squeeze the mixture into 16 compact, evenly sized balls. Using your palm, flatten each ball into a patty shape 2 inches in diameter, making the balls as uniform and flat as possible, but do not overwork or the cakes will be dry. (*Note:* If you aren't cooking the cakes right away, place on a baking sheet, cover loosely with plastic wrap, and refrigerate until ready to use.)

4. Heat 1$\frac{1}{2}$ tablespoons of the oil in a 12-inch nonstick skillet over medium-high heat. Fry the cakes in 2 batches. Fry for 2 to 3 minutes per side, until browned, adding a little oil if needed and using a spatula to flatten while cooking. Heat the remaining oil before adding the second batch. (*Note:* Watch the cakes carefully to prevent burning.) When done, drain briefly on paper towels. Transfer the cakes to a baking sheet and keep warm in a preheated 200°F oven while cooking the second batch. Serve hot on individual watercress-lined salad plates and pass with the chilled tartar sauce.

Entrees

Quick Scallion Spaghetti

Serves 4

This recipe is based on one of Italy's national dishes *spaghetti con aglio e olio* (spaghetti with garlic and olive oil), except I have replaced the garlic with scallions and added a grinding of fresh pepper and a sprinkling of Parmesan cheese. The scallions not only add crisp flavor but lovely color to this unpretentious, honest dish.

1 pound spaghetti

2/3 cup extra-virgin olive oil

Freshly ground pepper, to taste

6 ounces scallions, including greens, cut *very* thin on the diagonal

Freshly grated Parmesan cheese, to serve

1. Bring a 6- to 8-quart pot of lightly salted water to a boil over high heat. Add the pasta and return to a boil. Boil the pasta for 7 to 9 minutes, stirring occasionally, or until the pasta is *al dente* (slightly firm to the bite).

2. Two minutes before the pasta is ready, make the sauce: Heat the olive oil in a small heavy skillet over low heat. Remove the skillet from the heat, and season with pepper.

3. Working quickly, drain the cooked pasta, transfer back to the pot, add the sauce and scallions, and toss together. Serve at once, sprinkled with Parmesan cheese.

Penne with Italian Sausage, Peppers, and Onions

Serves 4 to 6

This dish is great for casual entertaining; just serve with crusty Italian whole-wheat bread from your local bakery. Because it is best when made a day or two ahead, you can really be relaxed when your company arrives.

Begin cooking the pasta ten minutes before the sausage sauce is done, so that everything will be ready at the same time. If you can't do this, then keep the cooked pasta warm over low heat in a colander set in a large pot with two inches of simmering water in the bottom. Cover the colander with aluminum foil. Though I doubt there will be any leftovers, they are wonderful sprinkled with additional Parmesan cheese and baked.

2	tablespoons olive oil
3	pounds fresh sweet Italian sausages, preferably made with fennel seeds (available at supermarkets or from a butcher), pricked all over with a fork to prevent sausages from bursting when cooked
1	large Spanish Sweet onion or 2 medium white onions, thinly sliced
2	green bell peppers, cored, seeded, and thinly sliced
	Two 16-ounce cans plum tomatoes, squeezed with hands, reserving juice
1	cup dry red wine
1/4	cup balsamic vinegar
3	tablespoons fennel seeds
1	tablespoon sugar
	Salt and freshly ground pepper, to taste
1	pound penne or rigatoni pasta
	Olive oil, as needed
	Freshly grated Parmesan cheese, to serve

Notes: The reason I lightly salt the water for cooking pasta is that it helps bring out the full flavor of the pasta, adding dimension to the dish.

Instead of cutting slippery canned plum tomatoes, just squeeze them with your hands into a bowl, which produces the same chopped result.

1. Heat 1 tablespoon of the oil in a heavy 12-inch skillet over high heat. Add the sausages and sauté for 6 to 8 minutes or until golden brown all over. Remove the skillet from the heat, and transfer the sausages to a cutting board. Holding the hot sausages with a fork, cut into $1/2$-inch-thick slices, transfer to a 6-quart nonreactive pot, and reserve until ready to use. Carefully drain the grease from the skillet.

2. Heat the remaining 1 tablespoon oil in the skillet over high heat. Add the onion and sauté for 3 minutes or until lightly golden brown. Stir in the bell peppers and sauté for 1 minute. Transfer the vegetables to the pot with the sausages.

3. Place the pot over medium-low heat. Stir in the tomatoes and their juice and bring to a boil. Stir in the wine, balsamic vinegar, fennel seeds, and sugar. Cook, partially covered, stirring occasionally, for 35 minutes. Season with salt and pepper. (*Note:* This dish can be prepared up to this point 2 days ahead. Let cool, cover, and refrigerate. Reheat before proceeding with the recipe.)

4. Prepare the pasta: Bring a 5-quart pot of lightly salted water to a boil over medium heat. Add the pasta, bring to a second boil, and boil, stirring occasionally, for 7 to 9 minutes or until the pasta is *al dente* (slightly firm to the bite). Drain in a colander, toss lightly with some olive oil, and cover to keep warm until ready to serve.

5. To serve, divide the pasta among dinner plates, ladle the sausage mixture over the top, sprinkle with Parmesan cheese, and serve hot.

Smoked Turkey and Leek Risotto

Serves 4

In Italy, risotto is served as a first course, but I find it makes a delightful one-dish lunch or supper. Rice, like pasta, has a sturdy texture and is extremely versatile as a base for a myriad of different accompaniments and flavors.

Adding liquid to arborio rice in small, frequent amounts, which it absorbs, and stirring constantly gives the grain a tender, creamy consistency.

In this soothing, yet piquant dish, the flavors of the smoked turkey and leeks complement one another, with the fresh color of spring coming from the leeks as well.

3 tablespoons olive oil

1 pound leeks, tough outer leaves removed, all but 2 inches of the greens removed, cut in half lengthwise, washed thoroughly, and thinly sliced

1 cup arborio rice (short-grain Italian rice, available at supermarkets or gourmet food stores) (*Note:* Do not rinse before cooking.)

3 cups canned low-sodium chicken broth (available at supermarkets), heated

$3/4$ cup dry white wine, heated

5 ounces skinless, boneless smoked turkey breast, available at supermarket deli counter or gourmet food stores, cut into $1/4$-inch-thick slices and julienned—cut crosswise into matchstick-sized strips

$1/2$ cup freshly grated Parmesan cheese (a 2-ounce piece)

Salt and freshly ground pepper, to taste

1. To make the risotto: Heat the olive oil in a heavy 5-quart saucepan over medium heat. Add the leeks and cook, stirring, for 3 to 5 minutes or until soft but not browned. Stir

in the rice and cook, stirring often, 3 minutes or until well coated and heated.

2. Stir in $1/2$ cup of the hot broth and all of the hot wine. (Stand back—the liquids will splatter.) Cook, stirring constantly, 3 to 5 minutes or until the liquid has been completely absorbed, but watch carefully to prevent the rice from sticking.

3. Add $1/2$ cup more of the hot broth and cook, stirring often, for 3 to 5 minutes or until most of the liquid has been absorbed—all but a few tablespoons so that the rice is unable to stick to the pan. Repeat the process 4 more times, adding broth in $1/2$-cup amounts and cooking, stirring frequently, until it is nearly absorbed. This will take a total of 20 to 25 minutes. (*Note:* Each addition of broth will take slightly longer to absorb. The more the rice cooks, the longer it takes to absorb liquid.) The rice should be creamy and *al dente,* slightly firm to the bite.

4. Remove the saucepan from the heat and stir in the smoked turkey and the Parmesan cheese. Cook, stirring often, for 2 minutes, just until the turkey is heated through. Season with salt and pepper and serve at once.

SPRING ONION BUFFET FOR 6

- Potted Herbed Cheese on French Baguette Rounds (page 69)
- Spring Vidalia Onion Pie (page 106)
- Mesclun Vinaigrette
- Sautéed Wild Mushrooms with Chopped Chives
- Onion-*Cassis* Sorbet (page 162)
- Fresh Strawberries
- Oniony Bloody Marys (add onion juice to taste to your favorite Bloody Mary recipe)

Spring Vidalia Onion Pie

Serves 6

(Dough can be made up to 2 days ahead.)

Quiche Lorraine is the classic French open-faced savory tart. However, this recipe is based on a variation of it—quiche Alsacienne—in which sautéed onions are added. Vidalia onions make the difference, binding together the filling ingredients as their sweetness absorbs the saltiness of the bacon. For further flavor, I have taken the liberty of adding a touch of mustard.

Dough

1 1/2 cups sifted unbleached all-purpose flour, plus more to dust

1   teaspoon salt

1/2 cup unsalted butter (1 stick), cut into small dice and chilled

1   large egg yolk lightly whisked with 2 tablespoons water

3 to 4 tablespoons ice water

1   tablespoon Dijon-style mustard

Filling

6   ounces thick slab bacon, cut into fine julienne strips

2   cups thinly sliced Vidalia, Maui, California Sweet Imperial, Texas 1015 SuperSweet, Walla Walla or other sweet mild onion, rings separated

1 1/4 cups heavy cream

3/4 cup 2% milk

4   large eggs

1/4 teaspoon salt

1/4 teaspoon freshly ground pepper

1/2 teaspoon ground mace

3/4 cup freshly shredded Swiss Gruyère cheese (a 2-ounce rindless piece)

1. To prepare the dough: Sift together the flour and salt in a medium bowl. Using a pastry blender or fork, cut in the chilled butter until the mixture resembles coarse crumbs. Stir in the egg yolk beaten with water until well blended. Then stir in the ice water, a few tablespoons at a time, as needed to allow the dough to form but not become sticky. Form into a flat disk, wrap tightly in waxed paper, and chill for 30 minutes.

2. On a lightly floured work surface, roll out the dough $1/8$ inch thick. Lightly moisten the edges of a 9-inch quiche pan or pie plate with water, and line the pan with the crust. Trim the crust to fit the pan with a 1-inch overhang. Gently press the crust up the sides of the pan, fold the overhang back over the inside crust, and crimp the edge decoratively. Brush the bottom of the crust with the mustard and prick the bottom all over with a fork. Lightly cover with plastic wrap and refrigerate until ready to use.

3. Preheat the oven to 400°F.

4. To make the filling: Fry the bacon in a heavy 10-inch skillet over high heat for 5 minutes or until crisp. Using a slotted spatula, transfer the bacon to a paper towel-lined plate to drain. Pour off all but 2 teaspoons of the bacon grease in the skillet.

5. In the skillet cook the onions over medium heat for about 6 minutes, stirring often, or until soft. Let cool completely and reserve.

6. Beat together the cream, milk, eggs, salt, pepper, mace, and cheese until well blended, and stir in the reserved onions. Place the quiche pan on an aluminum foil-lined baking sheet. Sprinkle the bacon on the bottom of the pie shell and pour the egg mixture over it, stopping at $1/8$ inch from the top to help prevent spillovers.

7. Bake in the middle third of the oven for 10 minutes. While the pie is still in the oven, reduce the heat to 350°F and bake for 50 to 60 minutes more, or until the filling is set, the top is golden brown and puffy, and the crust is crisp. (*Note:* Though the filling will become firmer as it cools, it should not jiggle loosely when the pan is jostled. If it does, the filling is not done.) Transfer the pie to a wire rack, and let stand for 10 minutes before slicing into wedges.

Tomato and Black Olive Onion Pizza

Makes one 12-inch pizza, serves 4, 2 slices each

Pizza is always an instant hit, and onion elevates this pizza to new heights. For those who have a penchant for pizza variations, this is a memorable one, with its generous topping of tomatoes and onion scattered with olives. On cue, the Parmesan cheese melts when the pizza is served.

As for making pizza dough, a timesaving product is Fleischmann's RapidRise yeast, a finely granulated, highly active strain of yeast, which obviates a first rising of the dough in favor of a 10-minute rest. Whether you use active dry or fast-working yeast, the electric mixer method below will work just fine. However, if you should opt for the quick-working yeast, then prepare the topping first, so that it is ready in time to crown the pizza.

Dough

2½ cups unbleached all-purpose white flour, plus more to knead

One ¼-ounce package active dry yeast or Fleischmann's RapidRise yeast

1 teaspoon sugar

1 teaspoon salt

1 cup very warm water (120°–130°F)

Olive oil, to grease bowl and pizza pan

Topping

1–1¼ pounds ripe tomatoes, preferably plum tomatoes, seeded and finely chopped

1 medium all-purpose yellow onion, very thinly sliced and rings separated

2 tablespoons extra-virgin olive oil

½ teaspoon freshly ground pepper

12 black brine-packed olives, such as Greek Kalamata olives, pitted and halved lengthwise (available at supermarkets)

⅓ cup freshly grated Parmesan cheese

1. To prepare the dough: In a medium bowl stir together 1½ cups of the flour, the undissolved yeast, sugar, and salt until well blended. Gradually add the very warm water, beating 2 minutes at medium speed with an electric mixer fitted with a paddle, scraping the sides of the bowl occasionally with a rubber spatula. Using a spoon, stir in enough of the remaining 1 cup all-purpose flour to make a soft dough. (*Note:* The dough will be very sticky.)

2. Transfer the dough to a liberally floured work surface and knead, making about 25 turns, adding more flour as needed, until the dough is smooth and elastic.

   Alternatively, attach a dough hook to your electric mixer, and beat on medium speed for 3 to 5 minutes, adding up to ¼ cup flour, until the dough is smooth, soft, and elastic, stopping often to scrape the sides of the bowl and let the dough cool.

3. Lightly grease a medium bowl with olive oil. Transfer the dough to the bowl and turn the dough once to coat it with the oil. Cover the top of the bowl with a towel and let stand in a warm, draft-free place about 1 hour or until doubled in size. (*Note:* If using RapidRise yeast, cover and let rest for just 10 minutes. This amount of time allows the

dough to relax, not rise.) Proceed with the recipe, but don't punch the dough down.

4. Meanwhile, prepare the topping: In a medium bowl combine the tomatoes, onion, olive oil, and pepper, and toss until well blended.

5. Preheat the oven to 425°F and lightly grease a 12-inch pizza pan.

6. Transfer the pizza dough to a lightly floured work surface and gently punch the dough down once. (*Note:* The dough can be frozen. Wrap tightly and freeze up to 1 month. When ready to use, thaw completely and proceed with Step #7.)

7. Transfer the dough to the greased pizza pan. Using your fingers (if necessary lightly flour them), press the dough so it spreads to the edge to form an even crust. Pinch the edge to form a $1/2$-inch-high rim.

8. Using a slotted spoon, transfer the topping to the dough and spread it over the dough to the edge. Scatter the olives over all. Bake in the lower third of the oven for 20 to 30 minutes or until the crust is crisp and golden. Sprinkle with the Parmesan cheese and serve.

AN AUTUMN PICNIC IN THE PARK FOR 4

- Tomato and Black Olive Onion Pizza (page 108)
- Antipasto
- Brownies
- Sparkling Mineral Water/Chianti

Company Brisket on a Bed of Onions

Serves 6

This melt-in-your-mouth brisket is a cinch to prepare, and though it takes five hours to bake, all of it is unattended cooking time. Low heat and a lot of onions are the keys to this prize-winning dish. In fact, three pounds of onions go into this, and it is just this bed of onions that infuses the meat with moistness and a wonderful flavor as it cooks. When done, onions and the meat juices create a lovely, mellow sauce.

2   tablespoons canola or vegetable oil

3   pounds all-purpose yellow onions, very thinly sliced

3   tablespoons paprika, preferably Hungarian (available at supermarkets)

One 4^1/$_2$-pound partially trimmed boneless beef brisket [*Note:* Brisket that is available at the supermarket or from the butcher typically comes packaged in Cryovac (a vacuum-sealed plastic package) and will have a thin, protective layer of fat—do not remove this.]

1^1/$_2$ teaspoons salt

2   teaspoons freshly ground pepper

1.   Preheat the oven to 300°F.

2.   Grease the bottom of a 6-quart Dutch oven or covered casserole with the canola oil. Add the onions and spread in an even layer. Sprinkle the onions with 1 tablespoon of the paprika. Place the brisket, fat side down, on top of the bed of onions. Season the top of the brisket with the salt and pepper and the remaining 2 tablespoons paprika and cover.

3.   Bake, covered, in the lower third of the oven for 3 hours. (*Note:* If necessary, add up to 2 cups warm water if there is not enough liquid to prevent the brisket from burning.)

4. Increase the heat to 350°F and bake, covered, for 2 hours more or until the brisket is *very* tender but not falling apart; however, you should almost be able to slice it with a fork. (*Note:* If necessary, add up to $\frac{1}{2}$ cup warm water if there is not enough liquid to prevent the brisket from burning.)

5. To serve, trim off the fat and discard. Cut the brisket diagonally across the grain into $\frac{1}{4}$-inch-thick slices and top with the onions and pan juices.

WINTER POT LUCK DINNER FOR 6

(You make the brisket and colcannon, and ask your guests to bring the rest!)

- Company Brisket on a Bed of Onions (page 111)
- Colcannon (page 133)
- Green Salad (comprising lettuce, cucumbers, and tomatoes) with Italian Dressing (bottled or homemade)
- Glazed Carrots
- French Dinner Rolls
- Beverages (preferably the soft variety)
- Gingerbread Cake with Whipped Cream or Vanilla Ice Cream

Beef Medallions with Shallots and Port Glaze

Serves 4

Tenderloin is a very special, expensive cut of beef, so I reserve this dish for a small elegant gathering of four or a romantic dinner for two, accompanied by a full-bodied red wine.

The tenderloin along with the sublime shallots and their glaze of ruby port and red currant jelly create an epicurean delight—fit for any gourmand. This is the only recipe in this entire cookbook that utilizes shallots whole; their graceful shape and singular taste are showcased in this preparation.

Glaze

1   tablespoon canola or vegetable oil

8   ounces small shallots, peeled and trimmed according to the directions on pages 48–49, but do not slice and be careful not to penetrate the interior, so that the shallots remain whole when cooked (*Note:* Choose shallots as similar in size as possible.)

$1/4$ cup ($1/2$ stick) unsalted butter (*Note:* Do not substitute margarine because the flavor of the sauce is at its best when butter-based.)

2   tablespoons sugar

$1/3$ cup ruby port

3   tablespoons red currant jelly

Beef

2   teaspoons canola or vegetable oil

$1 1/2$ pounds small beef tenderloin, trimmed of all fat (Ask butcher to cut into four 1-inch-thick slices, and to tie with string to form "medallions.")

Salt and freshly ground pepper, to taste

1. To make the glaze: In a heavy 10-inch skillet heat the oil over medium heat. Add the shallots and cook for 10 to 15 minutes, shaking the skillet frequently. (Do not stir or the shallots will fall apart.) Cook until deep golden brown all over, very tender but not falling apart.

2. Reduce the heat to low, and add the butter. Let melt, then sprinkle the sugar over the shallots. Cook about 10 minutes, shaking the skillet frequently, or until the mixture turns golden brown, watching carefully to prevent the shallots from burning.

3. Add the port and jelly—stand back because the liquid will splatter. Shake the skillet constantly until the shallots are

coated with a syrupy glaze. Cover to keep warm until ready to use, up to 20 minutes.

4. Preheat the oven to 375°F.

5. Meanwhile, prepare the beef: In a heavy 12-inch skillet heat the oil over high heat. Add the medallions and sear for 30 seconds on each side or until browned on the outside but still rare inside. Transfer to a 13 by 9 by 2-inch baking dish and bake for 5 to 13 minutes, depending on desired degree of doneness: 5 minutes for rare, 8 minutes for medium-rare, and 13 minutes for well done. (*Note:* The beef will continue to cook slightly even after being removed from the oven.)

6. Just before you are ready to serve, heat the glaze over very low heat, stirring often, until warm.

7. Working quickly, cut the strings off the medallions and season with salt and pepper. Place a medallion on each of 4 dinner plates, top with some of the pan juices, ladle glaze over the top, and divide the shallots among the servings. Serve at once.

Judith Lydic's Persian Roast Chicken
(Kababe Morg)

Serves 4

Judith Lydic is a chef friend of mine who lent me her recipe to use in this book. Judith has lived and traveled in many exotic lands, among them Lebanon, Iran, Afghanistan, Iraq, and Saudi Arabia. While living in Persia, her cook and friend, Rose, taught Judith many Persian delicacies, among them the following dish, which captures Persia's exceptional and distinctive culinary attribute of combining meat or poultry with fresh and dried fruit.

Onions are the base for the stuffing, and add dash and abundant texture, so this recipe was an obvious choice for inclusion in this cookbook. This dish is best when served with rice, preferably imported Iranian rice or other long-grain white rice. Mix the stuffing with the rice and serve alongside this wonderfully aromatic, beautifully colored chicken, drizzling any pan juices over all. I always hope for leftovers of this dish, which make a great boxed lunch for the office.

One 3- to 3$\frac{1}{3}$-pound roasting chicken or fryer

3   tablespoons unsalted butter

1   large Spanish Sweet onion or 2 medium all-purpose yellow onions, finely chopped

4   ounces dried apricots, finely chopped

2   ounces pitted dried prunes, finely chopped

$\frac{1}{4}$ cup raisins

$\frac{1}{4}$ cup dried currants

1   large unpeeled red apple, finely diced

1   teaspoon salt

$\frac{1}{2}$ teaspoon freshly ground black pepper

$\frac{1}{2}$ teaspoon ground cinnamon

2   teaspoons dried tarragon, crumbled

1   teaspoon dried thyme, crumbled

2   grams saffron threads, ground, to make $\frac{1}{2}$ tablespoon ground

Hot cooked Basmati rice (prepared according to package directions), to serve

1.   Clean, wash, and prepare the chicken as you would for roasting.

2.   In a heavy 12-inch skillet melt the butter over medium heat. Raise the heat to medium-high, add the onion, and sauté for 5 minutes. Stir in the apricots, prunes, raisins, currants, and apple and sauté for 5 minutes more or until the onions are tender.

3.   In a small bowl combine the salt, pepper, cinnamon, tarragon, thyme, and saffron and mix until well blended. Stir half the

seasoning blend into the onion mixture and let cool to room temperature. Reserve the remaining seasoning blend.

4. Preheat the oven to 350°F.

5. With your fingers, gently pull the skin away from the breast of the chicken. Run your fingers along the breast meat to release the membrane holding the skin to the breast. (*Note:* The objective is not to puncture or remove the skin, but to form a "pocket" in which you can rub the seasoning on the breast meat.) Rub half the seasoning blend between the breast meat and the skin. Press the skin against the breast and lightly rub the surface of the skin to smooth the seasoning underneath. Rub the entire outside of the chicken with the remaining seasoning blend.

6. Place the chicken, breast side up, on a rack (preferably non-stick) in a roasting pan. Lift the wings up toward the neck, then fold under the back of the bird so they stay in place. Stuff the chicken cavity with the cooled seasoned onion mixture, reserving any remaining stuffing to be served later, stirred into the rice accompaniment. Close up cavity by folding skin over the opening and skewer closed with metal trussing skewers. With butcher's twine, tie the legs together. Alternatively, use a stuffing clamp.

7. Insert a meat thermometer into the thickest part of the chicken between the breast and thigh, being careful that the pointed end of the thermometer does not touch the bone. Roast for 1 to 1½ hours (20 to 25 minutes per pound) or until the meat thermometer reaches 180°F and the thickest part of the drumstick feels soft when you press it. Let stand 10 minutes before carving. (*Note:* When serving, scoop out all the stuffing immediately after roasting and serve in a separate bowl. Never leave stuffing inside a poultry carcass, and always store any stuffing leftovers separately.)

Philippine-Style Pork and Chicken Stew

Serves 6 to 8

Among the traits that mark the cuisine of the Philippines is a pre-dilection for cooking several kinds of foods together in juxtapositions that are intriguing, albeit seemingly peculiar, to many Americans. The following recipe illustrates this approach, in its combination of chicken and pork.

Another aspect of this stew that makes it different from the traditional American repertoire is that the combination of ingredients is not organized around one central ingredient. Rather, each ingredient has equal status; no one flavor is singled out to dominate. Instead the combination itself determines the final taste.

Here is the perfect recipe for the "pot watcher" in your family. The scallions are added at the end of the cooking process for extra color, texture, and a spark of onion flavor. Together the ingredients make for a rousing and delightfully hearty stew.

2 tablespoons canola or vegetable oil

1 large Spanish Sweet onion or 2 medium white onions, finely chopped

$\frac{1}{2}$ small head green cabbage, tough outer leaves removed, cored, and very thinly shredded

$1\frac{1}{2}$ pounds skinless, boneless chicken breast, cut into $\frac{1}{2}$-inch-wide strips

$1\frac{1}{2}$ pounds boneless pork loin, trimmed and cut into 1-inch cubes

Three $14\frac{1}{2}$-ounce cans low-sodium beef broth

$\frac{1}{4}$ cup red wine vinegar

4 medium cloves garlic, minced

1 teaspoon salt, plus more to taste if necessary

$\frac{3}{4}$ teaspoon freshly ground pepper, plus more to taste if necessary

1 teaspoon paprika

$\frac{1}{2}$ teaspoon ground allspice

$\frac{1}{2}$ teaspoon ground ginger

$^1/_2$ cup coconut cream (available at supermarkets)

$^1/_3$ cup thinly sliced scallions, including greens (sliced on the diagonal)

Hot cooked brown or white rice (prepared according to package directions), to serve

1. Heat the oil in a heavy 6-quart nonreactive pot over medium-high heat until hot but not smoking. Add the onion and cabbage and sauté for 5 to 8 minutes or until the onion is a very light golden brown. Using a slotted spoon, transfer to a heatproof bowl and reserve. Add the chicken and sauté for 5 minutes or until opaque, then transfer to the bowl with the onion mixture. Add the pork to the pot and sauté for 7 to 10 minutes or until browned all over. Transfer the pork to the bowl with the onion-chicken mixture. Carefully pour off the excess fat, and return the pot to medium-high heat.

2. Stir in the broth, vinegar, and reserved onion, chicken, and pork mixture. Then stir in the garlic, salt, pepper, paprika, allspice, and ginger until well blended, and bring to a boil. Reduce the heat to low, cover, and simmer for 40 to 50 minutes, stirring occasionally, until the chicken and pork are very tender and no pink remains.

3. Put the coconut cream in a small bowl, whisk 1 cup of the hot stew into the bowl, then stir back into the pot. Stir in the scallions until well blended. Adjust the seasoning with more salt and pepper if necessary. (*Note:* The recipe can be made up to this point 2 days ahead. Let cool, cover, and refrigerate.) Serve the stew hot over cooked brown or white rice.

Lemon Sole with Roasted Garlic and Red Peppers in Parchment

Serves 4

Cooking *en papillote*—the French technique of cooking in parchment paper—is not only simple but makes a dramatic presentation as it retains the flavors of foods being cooked in that way. These paper packets are split open at the table, with the aromas of the foods within escaping, creating an alluring perfume. In this recipe, lemon sole steams in its own juices while it is infused with the natural flavors of roasted garlic and red peppers. The buttery garlic and the punch of red peppers enliven the delicately flavored sole, producing an altogether breathtaking dish.

Cooking with parchment makes for easy clean-up—no messy pans to wash after dinner! To save even more time, assemble the packages earlier in the day, refrigerate, and bake before serving. Just be sure to bring the packages to room temperature before baking.

2 tablespoons olive oil, for brushing

Four 6-ounce lemon sole fillets or orange roughy fillets

Salt and freshly ground pepper, to taste

One 2-ounce head Roasted Garlic (see page 141 for procedure), flesh removed and mashed with a fork to form a paste

3/4 cup finely chopped jarred roasted red peppers, drained (available at supermarkets)

1 medium lemon, cut into 4 wedges, to serve

1. Preheat the oven to 400°F.

2. Cut 4 sheets of cooking parchment paper, each measuring 12 by 16 inches. Fold each sheet in half and cut out a heart shape that's double the size of the piece of fish that you are baking. One by one, unfold the cutout, and brush the inner surface and edges with olive oil. Place a fillet on one side of

the fold almost in the center (closer to fold than edges), and season with salt and pepper. If necessary, fold under the small end of the fish fillet to make it fit. Spread the fillet evenly with one quarter of the mashed roasted garlic, then top with one quarter of the finely chopped roasted red peppers. Fold the paper over the fish to meet the other side. Fold an edge $1/4$-inch-wide along the open sides, overlapping each fold in pleats, as you work your way around. Make sure the package is tightly sealed to avoid leaks. Repeat with the remaining paper and ingredients.

3. Brush the surface of the packages evenly with olive oil. Divide the packages between 2 baking sheets and bake for 8 to 11 minutes until the parchment puffs up and browns slightly. To serve, slit open the packages: Watch out for the steam; it will burn. Serve at once accompanied by lemon wedges.

Grilled Tuna with Ginger-Shallot Zinfandel Sauce

Serves 4

The sauce recipe here is a takeoff on the time-honored ethereal French *beurre blanc* (white butter sauce). My addition of crystallized ginger adds a Caribbean note. Jamaica's ginger is world-famous; in fact, the island is sometimes called the land of ginger. Ginger in its many forms—fresh, dried and ground, and crystallized—finds its way into many Caribbean dishes, and sometimes crystallized ginger is eaten as a digestive after meals.

The natural sweetness of this sauce, imparted from the shallots and crystallized ginger, and hint of Zinfandel wine acts as an elegant background to fresh tuna steaks. The sauce is best, made just before serving, and its last-minute preparation is not only simple, but quick. However, it may be kept warm in a bowl set inside a larger bowl of warm water for up to 5 minutes.

Tuna

Four 6-ounce center-cut tuna steaks

Olive oil, to baste

Salt and freshly ground pepper, to taste

Sauce (Makes about 1 cup)

$^3/_4$ cup (1 $^1/_2$ sticks) unsalted butter, cut into small dice and chilled, plus 1 tablespoon butter

3 shallots, minced

3 tablespoons minced peeled fresh ginger root

$^1/_2$ cup Zinfandel wine

$^1/_4$ cup minced crystallized ginger (available at supermarkets)

Salt and freshly ground white pepper, to taste

1. Preheat the grill or broiler to medium-high.

2. To prepare the tuna: Lightly brush both sides of the tuna steaks with olive oil. Place the fish on the grill or on a broiler pan about 7 inches from heat source and cook for 4 minutes. Turn the tuna steaks over and grill or broil for 1 to 3 minutes more, depending on thickness, or until opaque but still springy to the touch. Tuna is best if cooked on the rare side and should have a pink center—a medium-rare doneness. (*Note:* Be careful not to overcook the fish; it will continue to cook slightly, even after being removed from the grill or broiler.) When the tuna is cooked, transfer to a platter, season with salt and pepper, and cover with aluminum foil to keep warm until the sauce is done.

3. To make the sauce: Melt the 1 tablespoon butter in a heavy nonreactive 2-quart saucepan over low heat. Stir in the shallots and ginger and cook about 4 minutes, stirring, or until the shallots are translucent.

Increase the heat to medium and add the wine. Bring the mixture to a boil, and boil until reduced by one-fourth, about 3 minutes. Strain the mixture through a fine-meshed sieve into a bowl, discarding the solids.

4. Return the strained mixture to the saucepan and place over very low heat. Whisk in the $^3/_4$ cup chilled butter, a bit at a time, whisking constantly and working on and off the heat, to prevent the mixture from coming to a boil, until all the butter is incorporated after each addition. (*Note:* The melted butter mixture should remain creamy, so that it has a velvety thickness with enough consistency to coat a spoon. It should be warm, but not so hot that the butter is separated into liquid butterfat and milk solids.) Stir in the crystallized ginger and season with salt and pepper. (*Note:* The sauce should be made just before serving.) Drizzle the sauce over the warm tuna steaks and serve at once.

SUMMER BARBECUE FOR 4

- Strawberry-Mango Salsa with Tortilla Chips (page 151)
- Grilled Swordfish with Texas 1015 SuperSweet Onion–Cilantro *Pesto* (page 123)
- Onion-Basil Bachelor's Biscuits (page 145)
- Corn on the Cob
- Praline or Butterscotch-Swirl Ice Cream with Hot Chocolate Sauce
- Lemonade/Beer/Sangria

Grilled Swordfish with Texas 1015 SuperSweet Onion–Cilantro Pesto

Serves 4

(*Pesto* can be made 1 day ahead.)

My combination of sweet onion, garlic, toasted walnuts, and fresh cilantro creates a spectacular and uniquely flavored Tex-Mex version of the traditional Italian basil-based *pesto*. The sweet onion juice adds a refreshing quality to this *pesto*, which provides an exciting counterpoint to the richness of swordfish.

Pesto (Makes about 2¼ cups)

1 cup finely diced Texas 1015 SuperSweet or another sweet mild onion

3 medium cloves garlic, crushed through a garlic press

1 cup (about 4 ounces) toasted walnuts (how-to procedure on page 164)

6 ounces fresh coriander (cilantro), well washed; use the stems but trim their ends

One 4-ounce rindless piece Parmesan cheese, freshly grated

¾ cup olive oil

Salt and freshly ground pepper, to taste

Swordfish

Four 6-ounce center-cut swordfish steaks

Olive oil, to baste

1. To make the *pesto:* Combine the onion, garlic, walnuts, coriander, and Parmesan cheese in the bowl of a food processor fitted with a metal blade. Process about 2 minutes or until

very finely chopped and well blended, scraping down the sides of the bowl as necessary.

2. With the machine running, gradually pour the olive oil in through the feed tube in a slow, steady stream until completely incorporated, scraping down the sides of the bowl as necessary. Season with salt and pepper. Cover and reserve at room temperature until ready to serve. (*Note: Pesto* can be made 1 day ahead. Cover and refrigerate. Stir before using at room temperature.)

3. Preheat the grill or broiler to medium-high.

4. To prepare the swordfish: Lightly brush both sides of the swordfish steaks with olive oil. Place the fish on the grill or on a broiler pan about 7 inches from the heat source and cook for 3 to 4 minutes. Turn the swordfish steaks over and grill or broil for 2 to 4 minutes more, depending on the thickness, or until opaque but still springy to the touch. (*Note:* Be careful not to overcook the swordfish; it will continue to cook slightly, even after being removed from grill or broiler.)

5. Serve at once topped with some of the *pesto*, and pass the remaining *pesto* for guests to help themselves.

Accompaniments

Baked Onions

Serves 6

Baked onions do take a while to cook, but some things can't be rushed. All you really have to do, though, is pop them in the oven. The heat forces the pre-cut onion sections to open up, causing them to look like the petals of a flower. Meanwhile, the texture loses its crunchiness and becomes supple, mellow with true onion flavor—a simple, old-fashioned culinary delight.

Onions

6 medium all-purpose yellow onions or other onions, about 3 inches in diameter (about 2¾ pounds)

Glaze

2 tablespoons unsalted butter or margarine, melted

2 tablespoons honey

1 tablespoon ketchup

1 teaspoon paprika

½ teaspoon salt

1. Preheat the oven to 400°F.

2. To prepare the onions: Cut a very thin slice from the root end of each onion so that it can stand upright, but don't penetrate into the interior of the bulb. Cut a very thin slice off the top to remove the stem. Peel, and cut an "X" 2 inches into each onion top. Arrange the onions, root ends down, in a baking dish that is large enough to hold them in one layer snugly; a 9-inch square baking dish works well.

3. To make the glaze: Combine the melted butter, honey, ketchup, paprika, and salt in a small bowl and stir until well blended.

4. Spoon the glaze evenly over the onions and "tent" the baking dish with aluminum foil. (Cover with foil, but do not let the foil rest on the glaze.) Bake the onions in the middle of the oven for 1 hour or until they test *very* tender when pierced with a fork. (*Note:* Cooking time may be longer, depending on the size of the onions.)

5. Spoon some of the glaze over each onion and serve hot as a side dish.

10 WAYS TO BAKE AN ONION

For each of the following variations, use the Baked Onions recipe as a springboard. Remember that cooking times may vary depending on the size of the onions you use.

Deviled Baked Onions

Follow the recipe on page 125 for preparing the onions. Omit the glaze and before baking spread each onion with 1 tablespoon Dijon-style mustard followed by a sprinkling of unseasoned bread crumbs (1/3 cup total). Bake as instructed. Just before serving, sprinkle each onion with a pinch of cayenne (ground red pepper).

Pesto-Topped Baked Onions

Follow the recipe on page 125 for preparing the onions. Omit the glaze and bake as instructed. Just before serving, divide 1 cup homemade or store-bought *pesto* (Italian basil sauce) over the onions.

Double-Hawaiian Baked Onions

Use Maui onions and follow the recipe on page 125 for preparing them. Substitute 1/2 cup coconut cream (available at supermarkets) for the glaze, spooning it over them before baking.

Citrus-Spiked Baked Onions

Follow the recipe on page 125 for preparing the onions. Omit the glaze and during the last 10 minutes of baking time divide 1 cup orange marmalade over the onions.

Indian-Style Baked Onions

Follow the recipe on page 125 for preparing the onions. Omit the glaze and during the last 10 minutes of baking time divide 1 cup mango chutney (available at supermarkets) over the onions.

Baked Onions with Red Pepper Sauce

Puree three 7-ounce jars of roasted red peppers, drained (available at supermarkets) in the container of a food processor fitted with a metal blade and season with salt and pepper. Follow the recipe on page 125 for preparing the onions. Omit the glaze and spoon the puree over the onions before baking.

Pizza-Parlor Baked Onions

Follow the recipe on page 125 for preparing the onions. Omit the glaze and ladle 3 cups homemade or store-bought tomato pizza sauce over the onions before baking. During the last 15 minutes of baking time, divide $1/2$ cup shredded part-skim milk mozzarella cheese evenly over the onions.

Baked Onions Florentine

Follow the recipe on page 125 for preparing the onions. Omit the glaze. Cook two 9-ounce packages frozen creamed spinach according to the package directions and ladle over the onions during the last 20 minutes of baking time.

Cowboy's Favorite (a full meal!)

Follow the recipe on page 125 for preparing the onions. Omit the glaze and during the last 20 minutes of baking time divide three $10^1/2$-ounce cans (3 cups) store-bought or home-made chili with or without beans over the onions.

Instant Sauced Baked Onions

Follow the recipe on page 125 for preparing the onions. Omit the glaze and divide two $10^1/2$-ounce cans Campbell's condensed French Onion Soup over the onions before baking.

Couscous with Apples and Shallots

Serves 6 to 8

Here I have delicately cooked the world's smallest pasta—Moroccan couscous—in chicken broth and studded it with apples, shallots, pine nuts, carrots, and golden raisins, with honey and fresh mint as further flavorings. The combination of apples and onions is a smooth one. Team this dish with chicken or pork, or serve it as is as a light main course. It cooks, steams in fact, in all of five minutes, making it a perfect last-minute side dish or light lunch.

Chop the fresh mint just before adding it to retain its gorgeous green color.

2¼ cups canned low-sodium chicken broth

2 tablespoons honey

One 10-ounce box Moroccan couscous (available at supermarkets)

4 ounces shallots, minced (see directions on page 53 for quick method of peeling)

2 medium red-skinned apples, such as Red Delicious or McIntosh, unpeeled and finely diced

½ cup golden raisins

½ cup pine nuts (*pignoli*) about 3 ounces, toasted on a baking sheet in a 350°F oven for about 8 minutes or until lightly golden

2 medium carrots, shredded using a food processor fitted with a shredding disk or the large-holed side of a box grater

¼ cup finely chopped fresh mint

Salt and freshly ground pepper, to taste

1. Heat the chicken broth and honey in a 4-quart saucepan over medium heat and bring to a boil. Stir in the couscous and cover. Remove the pan from the heat and let it stand for 5 minutes.

2. Stir in the shallots, apples, raisins, toasted pine nuts, carrots, and fresh mint until well blended. Season with salt and pepper.

3. To serve, transfer to a serving plate, with a fork, fluff lightly, and serve at once.

Deep-Fried Onion Rings with Mango Puree

Serves 4

Onion aficionados will agree that there is nothing like the conviviality inspired by sharing a basket of onion rings. If you are a traditionalist when it comes to this grand American dish, use ketchup instead of my unique mango puree.

This recipe presents the simplest method of preparing onion rings: Just dip the raw rings into milk, then dredge them in flour, which renders when they are deep fried a very thin and wonderfully crisp, flaky coating that allows the onions to peek through—a hint at the delicacy beneath.

1   large Spanish Sweet or California Sweet Imperial onion or Vidalia, cut into $1/4$-inch-thick slices and separated into rings

$2/3$ cup milk

1   cup unbleached all-purpose white flour

1   large ripe mango, peeled, pitted, and thickly sliced

3   quarts peanut oil, for deep frying

Salt and freshly ground pepper, to taste

1. Dip the rings first into a bowl of the milk, then into a bowl of the flour, shaking off any excess, and place them in a single layer on a sheet of waxed paper.

2. Place the mango slices in the container of a food processor fitted with a metal blade. Process about 1 minute or until

puréed. Transfer to a small glass serving bowl, cover, and set aside until ready to serve.

3. Heat the oil in an 8-quart pot over medium-high heat until a deep-fry thermometer reads 375°F. To test if the oil is hot enough, drop an onion ring into the oil; if it sizzles, the oil is hot enough.

4. Wearing flameproof mitts, deep fry the rings in batches. Do not crowd the pot and stand back—the oil will splatter. Fry for 2 to 3 minutes, turning after 1 minute, or until crisp and the edges turn golden brown. (*Note:* Be careful not to over-cook the onion rings as they will continue to cook slightly even after you remove them.) Using long-handled tongs, transfer the rings to a paper-towel-lined baking sheet and drain briefly. Remove the paper towels and transfer the baking sheet to a preheated 200°F oven to keep the rings warm until ready to serve.

5. Deep fry onion rings with the remaining ingredients, skimming the surface of the oil in between batches to keep it clean. Season the onion rings with salt and pepper just before serving, not before or the salt will break down the oil, and pass with the mango puree.

Southwestern-Style Scalloped Potatoes with Roasted Leeks and Cumin

Serves 6 to 8

The long, oval, dusty-brown Russet potato is the classic baking potato. In general, these heavy spuds have a higher starch content than boiling potatoes, making them the best choice for scalloped potatoes. When baked in this way, they develop an enticingly faint, cheese-like flavor.

Classically, scalloped potatoes are made with cream. However, I have created an updated version that employs half-and-half, cumin, jalapeño peppers, Monterey Jack cheese, and—for a sublime touch—leeks.

To prevent any discoloration, slice the potatoes just before you are ready to assemble the dish. You can do so while the leeks are roasting.

2   tablespoons unsalted butter, plus more to grease gratin dish, at room temperature

1½   pounds leeks, tough outer leaves removed, trimmed and all but 2 inches of the greens removed, cut in half lengthwise, washed thoroughly, and thinly sliced

3   jalapeño peppers, cut in half lengthwise, seeds and ribs removed and minced (see how to handle and prepare fresh chile peppers on page 97)

4   medium baking potatoes, washed thoroughly, peeled, and sliced crosswise into ⅛-inch-thick slices, using a food processor fitted with a slicing disk or *mandoline,* following manufacturer's directions

1   cup half-and-half, at room temperature

1   teaspoon salt

¾   teaspoon freshly ground pepper

1¼   teaspoons ground cumin

4   ounces Monterey Jack cheese, shredded (about 1¼ loosely packed cups)

1.   Preheat the oven to 400°F. Lightly grease a 2-quart gratin dish or baking dish with a little of the butter.

2.   Place the leeks on the bottom of the prepared gratin dish in a smooth, even layer. Bake in the middle third of the oven for 15 minutes.

3.   Remove the hot gratin dish from the oven, stir the leeks to redistribute, add the jalapeño peppers, then spread the mixture in the pan. Overlap the potato slices in layers on top of the leek mixture. In a small bowl, whisk together the half-and-half, salt, pepper, and cumin until well blended; then

pour mixture evenly over all. Sprinkle with the cheese and dot the 2 tablespoons butter evenly over the top.

4. Bake for 20 minutes. Reduce the heat to 350°F and bake for 50 to 60 minutes more or until the potato-leek mixture has absorbed most of the liquid and the edges of the potatoes are golden brown and crisp. Test for doneness: When a toothpick or skewer is inserted in the center of the mixture and meets no resistance, the potatoes are done. Serve hot directly from the dish.

Thanksgiving Creamed Onions Supreme

Serves 6

I replaced the traditional ingredient of cream with whole milk to lower the fat content of this classic recipe. At the same time, I heightened the flavor and gave it a modern twist with tomato paste and tarragon, creating an ultimate creamed onion recipe, hence the title "supreme."

If you are in a hurry over the holidays and don't have time to peel fresh pearl onions, you can substitute thawed frozen pearl onions and skip the first step.

20 ounces fresh pearl onions, unpeeled

3 tablespoons unsalted butter or margarine

3 tablespoons unbleached all-purpose white flour

2 1/2 cups milk, heated

2 tablespoons tomato paste

1 1/2 teaspoons dried tarragon, crumbled

Salt and freshly ground pepper, to taste

1/4 cup unseasoned dry bread crumbs

4 ounces rindless Swiss Gruyère cheese, shredded (about 1 1/4 cups), or Jarlsberg cheese (available at supermarkets or cheese shops)

1. Bring a 4-quart saucepan of water to a boil over medium heat. Add the pearl onions, bring to a second boil, and boil for 2 minutes. Drain at once in a colander and plunge into an "ice bath" (a bowl of ice water). Using a knife, peel and trim the ends, but leave the onions whole.

2. Preheat the oven to 400°F.

3. In a heavy nonreactive 3-quart saucepan melt the butter over low heat. Gradually whisk in the flour, whisking constantly until large bubbles appear, about 30 seconds. Cook 1 to 2 minutes, whisking constantly, but do not let the *roux* brown. Remove the pan from the heat and gradually pour in the hot milk, whisking the bottom and sides of the saucepan constantly, until blended and smooth. Return the pan to low heat and stir until thick, about 5 minutes. Stir in the tomato paste and tarragon until well blended. Stir in the onions and season with salt and pepper.

4. Spoon the mixture into a 2-quart gratin dish. Sprinkle with the bread crumbs and top with the cheese. Bake for 20 to 25 minutes or until the cheese is melted, bubbly, and lightly golden brown. Serve hot directly from the baking dish.

Colcannon

Serves 6 to 8

This simple and delicious dish reflects the Irish love for potatoes, onions, and cabbage. I like to serve colcannon on St. Patrick's Day, when these comforting mashed potatoes flecked with silky green leeks and cabbage threads make a spirited accompaniment to an entree like corned beef.

Though colcannon is traditionally made with kale, cabbage is frequently substituted. I have seen colcannon prepared without leeks, or simply with the white of the leeks. However, the following manner of preparation is my favorite.

Colcannon is generally served during Halloween in the south of Ireland, where trinkets—wrapped in a piece of wax paper and buried in the colcannon—are said to tell the recipient's fortune. Their messages include a button for bachelorhood, a thimble for spinsterhood, a ring for marriage within the year, and a coin for wealth.

> 5 loosely packed cups finely shredded Savoy cabbage or green cabbage (from $3/4$ pound cabbage)
>
> 2 medium leeks, tough outer leaves removed, trimmed and all but 2 inches of the greens removed, cut in half lengthwise, washed thoroughly, and thinly sliced
>
> $2^{1}/_{2}$ pounds baking potatoes
>
> 6 tablespoons ($3/4$ stick) unsalted butter, melted
>
> $1/2$ cup milk (2%, if desired), or more if needed, heated
>
> Salt and freshly ground pepper, to taste

1. Heat 2 cups water in a deep 12-inch skillet over high heat until it reaches a simmer. Add the cabbage and leeks and cook for 13 minutes, stirring often, or until tender. Drain, cover to keep warm, and reserve.

2. Peel the potatoes, and cut them into $3/4$-inch-thick slices. Place the potatoes in a 5-quart pot and add water to cover by 2 inches. Place the pot over medium-high heat, bring to a boil, and boil for 15 to 20 minutes or until tender. Drain well. Transfer the potatoes to a large bowl, and add the butter and milk. Mash with a potato masher until well blended and the potatoes are light and fluffy. Add more warm milk if needed for the desired consistency. Stir in the reserved cabbage mixture until well blended. Season with salt and pepper and serve at once.

Sweet-and-Sour Cipolline

Makes 3 cups

(Can be made up to 2 weeks ahead.)

In this recipe, small Italian onions, with flat tops and bottoms, simmer in a sweet-sour bath, which permeates their delicate flavor. The onions remain whole, making for a lovely presentation.

Serve with roasted pork or flavorful fish like tuna. These onions also make elegant picnic fare that begs to be served with dried sausages, cheese, and coarse mustard.

1 pound *cipolline* or substitute pearl onions, unpeeled

1/4 cup extra-virgin olive oil, preferably very flavorful

1/2 cup balsamic wine vinegar

2 cups water

3 tablespoons firmly packed dark brown sugar

1/4 cup dry sherry

1/2 teaspoon salt

1/2 teaspoon freshly ground pepper

One 4-ounce jar sliced pimientos, drained

1/4 cup finely chopped fresh mint

Salt and freshly ground pepper, to taste

1. Prepare the *cipolline* according to the directions on page 76. If you are using pearl onions, follow the same directions but when they have reached the second boil, boil for 30 seconds only. Using a knife, peel and trim the stem ends, and just the woody part of the root end, but don't cut into the onions or they will fall apart when cooked.

2. In a 1 1/2 quart nonreactive heavy saucepan combine the onions, olive oil, balsamic vinegar, water, brown sugar, sherry, salt, and pepper and stir until well combined.

3. Place the pan over medium heat and bring to a boil. Reduce the heat to low and partially cover the pan. Simmer, stirring occasionally, for 30 to 35 minutes or until the onions are very tender but not falling apart. Stir in the pimientos and mint until well blended, and season with more salt and pepper.

4. Let the onion mixture cool completely. Spoon the mixture into a nonreactive airtight container, and store in the refrigerator up to 2 weeks. Serve at room temperature. Use a slotted spoon. (*Note:* This recipe is at its best when made 1 day ahead, which allows the flavors to mingle.)

Meat-Stuffed Onions

Serves 6

Stuffed onions are fun and easy to make—not to mention delicious! Microwaving the onions before stuffing works well, but I don't recommend microcooking them after they have been stuffed because the onions and stuffing get soggy.

Onions

6 medium all-purpose yellow onions or other onions that are about 3 inches in diameter (about 2$^3/_4$ pounds)

Stuffing

8 ounces extra-lean ground beef

$^1/_4$ cup thinly sliced scallions

1 tablespoon ketchup

1 tablespoon Dijon-style mustard

$^1/_2$ teaspoon salt

$^1/_4$ teaspoon freshly ground pepper

$^1/_4$ cup unseasoned dry bread crumbs

1 large egg white

1. To prepare the onions: Cut a very thin slice from the root end of each onion so that it can stand upright, but don't penetrate the interior of the bulb. Cut a very thin slice off the top to remove the stem. Peel. Bring a 5-quart pot of water to a boil over high heat. Add the onions, reduce the heat to medium, and cook, covered, for 20 minutes or until the outer layers are just tender and translucent and the middle is crisp-tender, tender enough to be pierced with a fork but slightly resistant. Cooking time may be longer, depending on size of the onions. (*Note:* Be careful not to overcook the onions or they will fall apart when you try to hollow them out.) Drain in a colander and refresh under cold, running water to stop the cooking process.

   Alternatively, microwave the onions: Wrap each in a damp paper towel and microwave at 100% for 3 minutes or until the middle is crisp-tender. (*Note:* Microwave ratings vary; microcook time may be slightly longer or shorter. If so, cook in increments of 30 seconds until onion middle is crisp-tender.)

2. Make the stuffing: Combine the beef, scallions, ketchup, mustard, salt, pepper, bread crumbs, and egg white in a medium bowl and stir until well blended.

3. Preheat the oven to 350°F.

4. When the onions are cool enough to handle, slice a quarter of the onion off the top of the stem end, saving the tops for another use. Using a small, sharp knife, cut a small "X" into the center on the top of each onion, cutting $2/3$ of the way down into the onion. Using a teaspoon, hollow out the center of each onion (the center should pull out easily), leaving a $1/2$-inch-thick wall of three layers, saving the scooped flesh for another use. (*Note:* There should not be a hole in the bottom of any of the onion shells. If there is, then patch it with another piece of onion.)

5. Arrange the onions, root ends down, in a baking dish large enough to hold them in one layer snugly—a 9-inch square baking dish works well. Fill each onion with $1/3$ cup of the stuffing, using your fingers to pack it tightly, and smoothing the tops. Pour 1 cup of water around the onions. Cover the top of the dish tightly with foil.

6. Bake in the middle of the oven for 15 minutes. Remove the foil and bake for 20 minutes more or until the onions are completely tender and the top of the filling is dappled a light golden brown.

---

10 WAYS TO STUFF AN ONION

For each of the following variations, use the recipe for Meat-Stuffed Onions as a road map but replace that stuffing with one of these. Remember that depending on the size of the onion, cooking times and filling amounts may vary. (Also, be sure to cool all cooked fillings to room temperature before using as a stuffing.)

Stuffed onions make a great buffet item. Some other filling ideas are homemade or store-bought corned beef hash; homemade scalloped potatoes; drained, canned tuna; or pureed, drained, canned beets; or mashed potatoes combined with a little freshly grated Parmesan cheese.

George Washington's Favorite Onion
Legend has it that this is the way our first President loved to have his onions. This combination is marvelous around the holidays—as a side dish or as a festive garnish on the turkey platter. Follow the recipe on page 136, except substitute 2 cups prepared mincemeat (available at supermarkets) for the meat stuffing. Fill and bake as described.

Lone-Star Stuffed Onions
Stir together 2 cups thawed frozen corn kernels and 1 cup shredded Hot Pepper Monterey Jack cheese (available at supermarkets) (a 4-ounce piece) in a medium bowl. Follow the recipe on page 136. (Texas 1015 SuperSweets make an appropriate choice with this particular filling.)

Coming-Up-Apples Stuffed Onions
Stir together 2 cups homemade or prepared applesauce with $1/2$ teaspoon ground cinnamon in a medium bowl. Follow the recipe on page 136.

All-American Stuffed Onions

Prepare enough poultry stuffing mix according to the package directions to make 2 cups. Follow the recipe on page 136. (Let the stuffing cool to room temperature before using.)

Who-Can-Resist Rice?

Prepare enough rice pilaf mix according to the package directions to make 2 cups. Follow the recipe on page 136. (Let the stuffing cool to room temperature before using.)

Southern-Style Stuffed Onions

Prepare enough grits according to the package directions to make 2 cups. (To save time, "quick-cooking grits" are available at supermarkets.) Stir in 1 cup shredded sharp Cheddar cheese (a 4-ounce piece) into the hot grits until melted and well blended. Season with salt and freshly ground pepper. Follow the recipe on page 136. (Let the stuffing cool to room temperature before using.)

Chinese-Style Stuffed Onions

Prepare one 10-ounce package frozen Chinese-Style Stir-Fry Vegetables according to the package directions. (I like to use Birds Eye brand.) Follow the recipe on page 136. (Let the stuffing cool to room temperature before using.)

Thanksgiving Stuffed Onions

Here is another great holiday side dish or garnish for the turkey or ham platter. A lovely presentation: Alternate these onions with the poultry-stuffing-stuffed onions and mincemeat-stuffed onions. Drain two 16-ounce cans cut sweet potatoes. Transfer to a small bowl and mash with a fork. Follow the recipe on page 136.

German-Style Stuffed Onions

Stir together 1 cup drained prepared sauerkraut (available at supermarkets) and 1 cup drained crushed pineapple, saving the juice for another use. Season with salt and freshly ground pepper. Follow the recipe on page 136.

Corn-Muffin Filled Onions

Prepare enough packaged corn muffin mix batter for 1 dozen corn muffins. Follow the recipe on page 136 for stuffing onions (but use this batter for the filling); fill each onion 1/2 full. Do not add the water to the baking dish and do not cover the dish with foil. Bake the stuffed onions, uncovered, according to the oven temperature and baking time on the package of corn muffin mix.

Garlic-Pumpernickel Bread Pudding

Serves 6 to 8

Start with a fabled sweet comfort food—bread pudding—and imagine it with the surprising flavor of a New York Reuben sandwich, on the garlicky side. The result: garlic-pumpernickel bread pudding, and an excellent accompaniment to any beef entree, such as pot roast, brisket, or roast beef.

This dish is a perfect addition to a Halloween dinner menu, since—as legend has it—garlic will ward off vampires!

Butter, to grease baking dish

3   large eggs

1½ cups milk, at room temperature (2%, if desired)

6   cloves garlic, crushed through a garlic press

1   tablespoon Dijon-style mustard

¼ teaspoon salt

¼ teaspoon freshly ground pepper

1   tablespoon caraway seeds

1½ cups freshly shredded Swiss Emmentaler cheese or Appenzeller cheese (a 5-ounce rindless piece)

One 1-pound loaf sliced pumpernickel rye bread

1.   Preheat the oven to 375°F. Butter the bottom and sides of a 3-quart baking dish.

2.   In a medium bowl whisk together the eggs, milk, garlic, mustard, salt, and pepper until well blended. Stir in the caraway seeds and 1 cup of the cheese until well blended.

3.   Arrange the bread slices in overlapping layers on the bottom of the prepared baking dish. Pour the egg mixture evenly over the bread slices, and using a fork, press the bread slices

down to immerse them evenly in the mixture. Sprinkle the surface with the remaining $1/2$ cup cheese.

4. Bake for 35 to 40 minutes in the middle third of the oven or until set and the top is dappled golden brown. Cut into squares and serve hot directly from the dish.

Roasted Garlic

Serves 4, 1 head each

(Can be made up to 3 days ahead.)

In its raw form, garlic is crunchy and powerfully flavorful. When roasted, however, it becomes as smooth as butter and has a mild, nutty flavor. If you don't believe it, just try this recipe.

You can use roasted garlic where you would use raw garlic, but do so when you want to bring forth a sweeter, milder flavor. Add roasted garlic at the end of cooking a dish, rather than at the beginning of a preparation so that it does not lose its subtle flavor by being overcooked.

Once roasted garlic is peeled, you can mash it with a fork to form a paste and use it to add marvelous flavor to a number of foods, such as dressings, soups, and sautéed vegetables.

Four 2-ounce whole heads garlic, unpeeled

$2^{1}/_{2}$ tablespoons olive oil

French baguette, to serve

1. Preheat the oven to 325°F.

2. Place the garlic in a small shallow baking dish. Evenly distribute the olive oil among the bulbs, rubbing each entirely with oil.

3. Bake in the middle third of the oven for 1 to $1^{1}/_{2}$ hours or until the heads are very soft when pierced with a fork. If

serving the bulbs whole, let cool enough to handle, and suggest diners break off the garlic cloves and squeeze and spread them over slices of French bread. (The garlic will slip out easily.) If using the roasted garlic as an ingredient, let the garlic cool enough to handle, break off the cloves, cut off the tip of each clove, and pinch the base of each clove to release the garlic into a bowl, cover, and refrigerate. [*Note:* A "Terra-cotta Garlic Baker" is a recent specialty item now available at gourmet shops such as Williams-Sonoma (page 79). The bakers are available in a range of sizes: some hold 1 head of garlic, others up to 8 heads. This item makes for very tasty roasted garlic; just follow manufacturer's directions on the package for cooking temperature and time.]

Breads and Condiments

Sun-Dried Tomato Garlic Bread

Makes 1 loaf

Sun-dried tomatoes started out as a fad, then became a trend, and now are here to stay. In this modern rendition of garlic bread, the ratio of butter to garlic is a lot less than in the classic version. Sun-dried tomatoes and garlic, accented with just a little butter, combine to form a paste that is spread on crusty Italian bread. Serve this on St. Valentine's Day—and succumb to the ruby color of the paste and the possibility of garlic being an aphrodisiac . . .

¾ cup drained oil-packed sun-dried tomatoes, 2 tablespoons of the oil reserved

8 cloves garlic, crushed through a garlic press

3 tablespoons unsalted butter, at room temperature

Salt and freshly ground pepper, to taste

1-pound loaf day-old Italian bread (about 15 inches long), cut crosswise on the diagonal at 1-inch intervals, stopping ½ inch from the bottom of the loaf (do not cut all the way through the bread)

1. Preheat the oven to 350°F.

2. Combine the tomatoes and the reserved oil, garlic, and butter in the bowl of a food processor fitted with a metal blade. Process about 2 minutes, scraping down the sides of the bowl as necessary, or until the mixture is fairly smooth and paste-like. Season with salt and pepper.

3. Place the loaf on an aluminum foil-lined baking sheet. Using your fingers, gently spread open the slices, but do not pull

them apart. Spread the tomato mixture evenly between the slices.

4. Bake in the middle third of the oven for 10 minutes or until the bread is heated through and the crust is crispy. If the crust becomes too brown, tent the bread loosely with aluminum foil. Serve at once.

Cranberry Corn Bread with Onion

Makes 1 loaf

(Can be made up to 3 days ahead.)

This is a moist, savory loaf—a striking contrast in flavors, colors, and textures. Here are the tastes of Thanksgiving all rolled into one. It makes a fancy sandwich bread especially appropriate with turkey. Or toast the bread, then cube it for croutons to grace a salad. The bread can also be served alongside a main course of roasted chicken or pork.

Vegetable oil cooking spray, to grease loaf pan

1 1/4 cups yellow cornmeal

1   cup all-purpose flour

1   tablespoon sugar

2   teaspoons double-acting baking powder

1   teaspoon baking soda

3/4 teaspoon salt

1   extra-large egg, lightly beaten

1   extra-large egg white

1   cup milk (2%, if desired)

1   cup finely chopped all-purpose yellow onions (about 2 medium)

2   teaspoons finely chopped fresh thyme or 3/4 teaspoon dried thyme, crumbled

3/4 cup dried cranberries (available at gourmet food stores)

1.   Preheat the oven to 350°F. Lightly grease a 9 by 5 by 3-inch loaf pan.

2.   In a medium bowl, stir together the cornmeal, flour, sugar, baking powder, baking soda, and salt until well blended.

3.   Stir in the egg, egg white, and milk until well blended. Fold in the onion, thyme, and cranberries until well combined.

4.   Transfer the batter to the prepared loaf pan. Bake in the middle third of the oven for about 45 minutes or until the surface is golden brown and a toothpick or cake tester inserted in the center comes out clean.

5.   Let stand in the pan for 10 minutes before slicing in the pan and serving warm. Or, transfer to a wire rack to cool completely. Can be covered and refrigerated up to 3 days.

Onion-Basil Bachelor's Biscuits

Makes 20 biscuits

I call these "bachelor biscuits," because even if you are cooking for only one, you'll want to make these often, especially since they are easy and delicious. You simply "drop" the batter on the baking sheet—no kneading, rolling, or cutting!

The small, delicate, savory biscuits make a splendid addition to teatime or a tasty finger food for your next barbecue. Serve them right out of the oven to capture their oniony flavor and melt-in-the-mouth texture.

2   cups unbleached all-purpose white flour

1   tablespoon double-acting baking powder

$1/2$ teaspoon salt

$1/3$ cup all-vegetable shortening

1   cup milk (2%, if desired)

²/₃ cup finely chopped red onion or substitute a sweet mild onion, such as Maui, California Sweet Imperial, Vidalia, Texas 1015 SuperSweet, or Walla Walla

2 tablespoons finely chopped fresh basil (*Note:* Do not substitute dried.)

1. Preheat the oven to 450°F.

2. In a medium bowl stir together the flour, baking powder, and salt until well combined. Using a pastry blender or fork, cut in the shortening until the mixture resembles coarse cornmeal.

3. Make a well in the center of the mixture and pour in the milk. Stir just until the dough clings together and no white specks are visible. Fold in the onion and basil just until blended. (*Note:* The batter will be thick and quite a few lumps may remain.)

4. Drop the dough in heaping tablespoonfuls onto an ungreased baking sheet, leaving 1 inch between the biscuits. Bake for 10 to 12 minutes or until flecked with brown. Serve at once.

Cardamom-Shallot Muffins with Currants

Makes 1 dozen

Cardamom is a favored spice in many exotic cuisines, including those of India and parts of the Middle East. These unusual muffins have a heady aroma from the shallots and cardamom, while the cardamom gives them a lemon-like flavor. They make a marvelous quick dinner bread, an excellent companion to beef, lamb, or chicken. Try them, too, with a hearty vegetable soup or bountiful green salad.

A friend of mine recently remarked that "You have to be a chemist to pick out flour nowadays!" There is a lot of truth in her statement, because it is hard to know which flour to buy for a particular recipe.

When I need an all-purpose flour, I choose unbleached white flour, rather than bleached white flour, because the bleaching process is a chemical shortcut. (Producers use chlorine to whiten the flour, rather than letting the naturally yellow fresh-ground white flour lighten slowly with exposure to air.) Also, be careful not to buy unbleached "self-rising" flour for this recipe as it contains sodium bicarbonate (used in baking powder) and salt.

Vegetable oil cooking spray, to grease muffin tin

2   cups unbleached all-purpose white flour

2   teaspoons double-acting baking powder

1   teaspoon salt

1   tablespoon sugar

1 1/2 teaspoons finely ground cardamom (available at gourmet food stores) (see Note below)

1   cup milk

6   tablespoons (3/4 stick) unsalted butter or margarine, melted

2   large eggs, lightly beaten

9   ounces shallots (for quick method of peeling see directions on page 48), finely chopped

2/3 cup dried currants or 1/2 cup seedless raisins

Note: If you are unable to purchase ground cardamom, you can prepare it at home from loose cardamom seeds that are available at Indian grocery stores. Alternatively, purchase cardamom pods and remove the seeds from the pods yourself before grinding the seeds in an electric spice grinder until finely ground.

1. Preheat the oven to 400°F. Lightly oil two 6-cup muffin tins, or one 12-cup muffin tin (each pan with cups of about 1/2-cup capacity).

2. In a medium bowl combine the flour, baking powder, salt, sugar, and cardamom and stir until well blended. Make a well in the mixture and pour in the milk, melted butter, and

eggs. Stir just until the batter clings together and no white specks are visible. (*Note:* The batter will be lumpy.) Stir in the shallots and currants just until blended.

3. Spoon the batter into the prepared muffin cups, dividing it evenly. Bake in the middle third of the oven for 15 to 20 minutes, or until the tops are dappled a light golden brown and a toothpick or cake tester inserted in the center comes out clean. (*Note:* Be careful not to overbake; the muffins will be more white than golden brown when done.)

4. Let the muffins stand in the tins for 5 minutes so that they will be less fragile and easier to remove. Remove the muffins by gently lifting each out with a blunt dinner knife. Serve hot.

Caraway-Rye Surprise Rolls

Makes 16 rolls

In this recipe moist rolls loaded with the earthy character of rye and graham flour have a surprise filling—garlic and onions. A molasses glaze adds a dark sheen to the rolls, a lovely finishing touch, and as they bake creates a marvelous scent throughout your home.

I use organic whole-grain rye flour obtainable from my farmers' market or a health food store. You can also buy rye flour from your supermarket, which is usually a mixture of light and dark flours (called medium rye flour). And since rye flour typically has very little gluten in it, I have added a small amount of rich, sweet whole-wheat graham flour to the dough. Unlike unbleached white flour, both rye and graham flour should always be stored tightly covered in the freezer to prevent the oils from becoming rancid.

If you decide to use the quick-acting kind of yeast, prepare the filling before beginning Step #1 so that it is ready when it comes time to fill the rolls.

Dough

1 cup whole-grain rye flour

$\frac{1}{2}$ cup whole-wheat graham flour

2 cups unbleached all-purpose white flour, plus more to knead and dust work surface

One $\frac{1}{4}$-ounce package active dry yeast or Fleischmann's RapidRise yeast

1 teaspoon sugar

1 teaspoon salt

2 tablespoons caraway seeds

1$\frac{1}{2}$ cups very warm water (120°–130°F)

2 tablespoons molasses

Filling

3 tablespoons extra-virgin olive oil, plus more to grease bowl and baking sheets

3 cups finely chopped all-purpose yellow onions (3 to 4 medium)

3 medium cloves garlic, crushed through a garlic press (*Note:* If you have only large garlic cloves, use 2; otherwise the flavor will overpower the onion filling.)

1 teaspoon salt

2 tablespoons molasses beaten with 2 tablespoons olive oil and 2 tablespoons hot water, to glaze

1. To prepare the dough: In a medium bowl stir together the rye flour, whole-wheat graham flour, 1 cup of the white flour, undissolved yeast, sugar, salt, and caraway seeds until well blended. Gradually add the very warm water and the 2 tablespoons molasses, beating with an electric mixer fitted with a paddle on medium speed for 2 minutes and scraping the sides of the bowl occasionally with a rubber spatula.

Using a spoon, stir in enough of the remaining 1 cup white flour to make a soft dough.

2. Transfer the dough to a lightly floured work surface and knead it, making about 50 turns until smooth, soft, and elastic.

Alternatively, attach a dough hook to your electric mixer, and beat on medium speed for 7 to 10 minutes, adding up to $1/3$ cup flour until the dough is smooth, soft, and elastic, stopping often to scrape down sides of bowl. Let the dough cool.

Lightly oil 2 baking sheets, and set aside.

3. Lightly grease a medium bowl with olive oil. Transfer the dough to the bowl and turn it once to coat it with the oil. Cover the bowl with a towel and let stand in a warm, draft-free place for 1 hour, or until doubled in size. (*Notes:* If using RapidRise yeast let rest just for 10 minutes. The dough will not double in bulk; this process is just to let dough relax, not rise.) Proceed with the recipe.

(The dough can be frozen at this point. Punch down once, wrap tightly, and freeze. Thaw before proceeding with the recipe.)

4. Make the filling: In a heavy 10-inch skillet heat the 3 tablespoons olive oil over high heat. Add the onion and sauté about 6 to 10 minutes or until soft and lightly golden brown. Stir in the garlic and salt and sauté for 1 minute more. Set aside and let cool completely before using.

5. Transfer the dough to a liberally floured work surface and divide into 16 evenly sized pieces (do not knead or punch down). Shape each piece into a ball. With lightly floured hands, one at a time, press your thumb 1 inch down into the center of the bottom of each ball and spread the roll open with your thumb, index, and middle finger to form a pocket. Fill the pocket with 1 heaping teaspoon of the filling, firmly packing it into the pocket. Pinch the sides of the

dough up, gathering in the center to cover the filling. Pinch and twist the gathered dough to create a tight, compact, round ball, being careful not to tear the dough. (*Note:* Make sure that the filling is entirely enclosed or it will burst through as the rolls bake.)

6. Transfer the rolls, seam side down, to the prepared baking sheets, placing them about 2 inches apart. Cover loosely with plastic wrap and let stand about 30 to 45 minutes in a warm, draft-free place or until doubled in size.

7. Preheat the oven to 425°F.

8. Gently brush the surface of each roll with some of the molasses glaze. Bake the rolls in the middle third of the oven for 10 minutes. Carefully remove from the oven and glaze again. Return to the oven and bake for 5 minutes more or until golden brown and crusty. Serve hot or at room temperature.

Strawberry-Mango Salsa

Makes about 4 cups

Here, a surprising fruit medley is salsa-fied with onions, lime, and cilantro to become a refreshing, kicky condiment. A small amount of sugar helps draw out the flavors of the fruit. This salsa is a wonderful accompaniment to chicken or fish, but my friends seem to most enjoy dipping tortilla chips into it. The texture and flavor—not hot, not sweet—contrast fantastically with the crunchiness and saltiness of the crisp chips.

I like to use Walla Walla onions for this dish, which should be made close to serving time, for the fruits do not keep. If last-minute preparation is not convenient, then cut the ingredients ahead of time and refrigerate them, then toss together 20 minutes before serving. This is a great portable dish—along with a bag of tortilla chips—for the next pot-luck dinner you are invited to.

1 large ripe mango, peeled, pitted, and cut into ¹/₂-inch dice

12 ounces ripe strawberries, hulled and quartered lengthwise

1¹/₂ cups finely chopped red onion or sweet mild onion, such as Maui, California Sweet Imperial, Vidalia, Texas 1015 SuperSweet, or Walla Walla

2 tablespoons sugar

¹/₄ cup fresh lime juice (2 to 3 small limes)

3 tablespoons minced fresh coriander (cilantro)

In a medium nonreactive bowl combine the mango, strawberries, onion, sugar, and lime juice and stir gently until well combined. Cover, and let stand at room temperature for 20 minutes to macerate. Stir in the coriander. Serve with a slotted spoon.

Banana Jam

Makes five ¹/₂-pint jars

I like to use red onions for this spicy rich condiment. While the flavor of the onions stabilizes the sweet and spicy ingredients, they still need time to harmonize, so make the jam at least one day before serving. Banana Jam has surprising uses. Try it as a topping on roasted meat, like pork; or on firm, white fish—it is particularly tasty on monkfish, with its lobster-like flavor. As a dip, place cream cheese on a brightly colored plate, spoon banana jam over it, and serve with wheat crackers.

This jam is the most difficult recipe in this book and requires special handling in preparation and storage. Cooking sugar is challenging and will need your undivided attention. Before you start, therefore, be sure to have all the ingredients prepared and waiting on the counter. For the procedure to sterilize canning jars, see page 155. Remember, too, that this jam must be refrigerated—even unopened—so write "To Be Refrigerated" both on the jam jar labels and on the outside of gift packages. Then wait for the rave reviews.

1½ cups firmly packed dark brown sugar

⅓ cup dark corn syrup

1 teaspoon Dijon-style mustard

1 teaspoon curry powder

½ teaspoon ground cloves

½ teaspoon black pepper

¼ cup apple cider vinegar

2 cups finely chopped red onion or sweet mild onion, such as Maui, California Sweet Imperial, Vidalia, Texas 1015 SuperSweet, or Walla Walla

2½ pounds ripe bananas (about 7 large), cut in half crosswise, then cut into ¼-inch-thick slices

1 teaspoon salt

1. Add the sugar to a heavy 6-quart nonreactive saucepan over medium-high heat. Heat, stirring *constantly,* for 4 to 6 minutes, just until it melts.

2. Remove from the heat and stir in 3 tablespoons water (stand back—the liquid will splatter), stirring constantly to dissolve any caramel sticking to the pan and prevent scorching. Return to medium-high heat and bring to a boil, stirring constantly. Then stir in the corn syrup, mustard, curry powder, cloves, and black pepper. Stir in the vinegar. Be careful—the mixture will splatter violently and the fumes will be *strong.* Add the onion and bananas. Return to a boil, stirring often, and boil for 3 minutes, stirring often.

3. Remove from the heat and stir in the salt until blended. Ladle the jam immediately through a wide-mouthed funnel into hot, sterilized jars, filling each to within ½ inch of the top. Wipe the rims with a dampened clean cloth and seal the jars with sterilized lids.

4. Using a jar lifter or tongs, put the jars in a water-bath canner or on a rack set in a deep kettle. The jars should not touch

each other. Add enough hot water to cover the jars by 2 inches and bring to a boil. Boil the jars, covered, for 5 minutes. With tongs or a jar lifter transfer them to a wire rack to cool. (*Note:* If using glass jelly jars with metal lids as opposed to Mason-type jars with rubber rings, you will hear the lids "ping" as they cool and the seals tighten.) Cool the jars completely and store in the refrigerator (even unopened).

Garlic Rosemary Jelly

Makes four ½-pint jars

This jelly is delicious spread on bagels with cream cheese or as a filling for an omelet for brunch. And one of my favorite cocktail party hors d'oeuvres is this jelly simply spooned over a small wheel of Brie or ripe Camembert cheese. If you like to make gifts for the special people in your life, this fragrant combination makes a very nice one. This jelly is best when fresh rosemary is used. (This recipe is courtesy of *Gourmet.* Copyright © 1994 by The Condé Nast Publications Inc.)

1¾ cups dry white wine

¼ cup white wine vinegar

⅓ cup finely chopped garlic

¼ cup finely chopped fresh rosemary leaves

3½ cups sugar

3-ounce pouch liquid pectin

1. In a kettle stir together well the wine, vinegar, garlic, rosemary, and sugar and bring the mixture, stirring constantly, to a rolling boil over high heat. Stir in the pectin quickly and bring the mixture back to a full rolling boil. Boil the jelly, stirring constantly for 1 minute, then remove the kettle from the heat.

2. Skim off any foam from the surface of the jelly and immediately ladle through a wide-mouthed funnel into four hot sterilized 1/2-pint jars, filling each to within 1/8 inch of the top. Wipe the rims with a dampened clean cloth and seal the jars with sterilized lids.

3. Using a jar lifter or tongs, put the jars in a water-bath canner or on a rack set in a deep kettle. The jars should not touch each other. Add enough hot water to cover the jars by 2 inches and bring to a boil. Boil the jars, covered, for 5 minutes. With tongs or a jar lifter transfer the jars to a wire rack to cool. [*Note:* If using glass jelly jars with metal lids (as opposed to Mason-type jars with rubber rings), you will hear the lids "ping" as the jars cool and the seal tightens.] Let the jars cool completely and store in a cool, dark place. Refrigerate after opening.

TO STERILIZE JARS FOR PICKLING AND PRESERVING

Wash jars in hot suds and rinse in scalding water. Put jars in a kettle and cover with hot water. Bring water to a boil, covered, and boil jars 15 minutes from the time that steam emerges from the kettle. Turn off heat and let jars stand in hot water. Just before they are to be filled invert jars onto a kitchen towel to dry. (Jars should be filled while still hot.) Sterilize jar lids for 5 minutes, or according to manufacturer's instructions.

Capunatina

Makes about 10 cups

Native to Sicily, *capunatina* is one of my favorite dishes. It has an assertive but delightful aroma and flavor, a blend of vegetable essences smoothed by olive oil and spiked with capers. Although *capunatina* can be served warm, it is usually served at room temperature or as a cold *prima piatti* (Italian first course—similar to an American appetizer course). This versatile food can be a savory snack, too; a typical Sicilian sandwich consists of a small loaf of bread hollowed out and filled with *capunatina*.

The recipe below comes from my friend Francesca Trubia's family in Sicily. The Trubias serve *capunatina* during the holidays, so they like to make enough for a large gathering. Francesca suggests frying the eggplant the day before to allow the excess oil to drain off before the rest of the ingredients are cooked. *Capunatina* is the kind of dish that really benefits from being made a day or two in advance; the flavors will truly marry. However, if you must serve the dish the day you make it, then she advises frying the eggplant early in the day, allowing it to drain for at least six hours.

The flavor of onion anchors this dish and is complemented by the flavor of eggplant, with their milder taste. Always look for small male eggplants, as they have a less bitter taste than the female plants. You can usually tell the difference. The purple male eggplant is more bulbous in shape than the female; the slender, purple female eggplant generally has tiny raised bumps, the size of freckles, near the stem.

$3/4$ cup extra-virgin olive oil, plus more if needed to fry eggplant

2 medium eggplants (about 2 pounds), unpeeled and cut into $1/2$-inch dice

4 tablespoons extra-virgin olive oil

1 large Spanish Sweet onion or 2 large white onions, coarsely chopped

4 ribs celery, coarsely chopped

One 6-ounce can tomato paste

4 large whole leaves fresh basil

1 teaspoon salt, or more, to taste

$3/4$ cup red wine vinegar

3 tablespoons sugar

$1/2$ cup drained capers

1 cup green Italian olives stuffed with pimientos or Spanish pimiento-stuffed olives, coarsely chopped

Crusty Italian bread, to serve

1. Heat ¼ cup of the olive oil in a deep nonreactive 12-inch skillet over medium heat until smoking. (*Note:* You will need to add more olive oil as you fry the eggplant to prevent it from sticking; it will absorb quite a bit of oil.) Fry the eggplant in 3 batches 8 to 10 minutes per batch or until lightly browned and tender, but not falling apart, adding another ¼ cup olive oil between each batch. Drain the eggplant, covered, in a large colander with a dish underneath for at least 6 hours, preferably overnight in the refrigerator.

2. Heat the 4 tablespoons olive oil in the skillet over high heat. Add the onion and celery and sauté them for 7 to 9 minutes or until the onion is translucent and the celery is crisp-tender.

3. Reduce the heat to low and stir in the tomato paste, basil, salt, vinegar, and sugar. Simmer the sauce, stirring occasionally, for 10 minutes. Stir in the capers and olives and cook for 10 minutes more, stirring occasionally. Gently stir in the drained eggplant until well blended and cook, stirring gently occasionally, until heated through, about 15 minutes.

4. Let cool to room temperature and serve with Italian bread. Or store in the refrigerator in an airtight glass container for up to 1 week.

Desserts and Candies

Warm Spiced Poached Pears with Raspberry Sauce and Chive Flowers

Serves 4, 1 pear each

Here is an elegant, simple dessert, ornamented with the lovely, lavender-colored, edible flowers of the chive plant. Be careful when peeling and coring the pears to ensure a pretty result. If you don't own an apple corer, then use a non-swivel vegetable peeler to partially core the pears. Just insert the point of the peeler into the bottom of the pear (next to the papery star shape of the root end) about ¾ inch down, rotate, and pull the piece out.

A Bosc pear has a matte, brownish-yellow skin and an exaggerated, slender, elongated neck. Choose pears that are similar in size, with level bottoms so that they can stand upright on a dessert plate.

The aroma of the poaching liquid is intoxicating—so much so that I have been known to simmer it in my kitchen (without the sugar or pears) as a room fragrance during the winter entertaining months!

4 slightly underripe Bosc pears

½ cup fresh lemon juice (3 to 4 medium lemons), the halves reserved for rubbing on the pears

4 cups water

1½ cups sugar

One 3-inch-long piece of lemon zest (all white, spongy bitter pith removed)

One 6- to 7-inch-long vanilla bean, cut in half lengthwise

2 whole cinnamon sticks

8 whole cloves

Six ¼-inch-thick slices fresh ginger root

One 10-ounce package frozen raspberries, thawed

2 tablespoons sugar

4 fresh pesticide-free chive flowers, the petals pulled from the flower head, to garnish

Sweet dessert cheese, such as L'explorateur or St. André, to serve (optional)

Sweet crackers, such as Carr's Wheatmeal, to serve (optional)

1. Peel and core each pear from the bottom, keeping the pear whole and the stem intact. Rub each pear with the reserved lemon halves to prevent discoloration.

2. Combine the water, sugar, lemon juice, lemon zest, vanilla bean, cinnamon sticks, cloves, and ginger in a 5-quart non-reactive saucepan over high heat. Stir the mixture until well blended and bring to a boil. Reduce the heat to low, cover, and simmer for 30 minutes. Strain the liquid through a fine-meshed strainer into a bowl, discard all the solids, and return the liquid to the saucepan.

3. Place the pears in the saucepan in their side, and place the pan over low heat. Cover and poach the pears for 15 to 20 minutes, turning the pears once halfway through the cooking time, and basting often with the juices, or until just tender. Test for tenderness by piercing with a knife. (*Note:* If the pears are too underripe, cooking time could take up to 50 minutes.)

4. Meanwhile, combine the raspberries and the 2 tablespoons sugar in the bowl of a food processor fitted with a metal blade and process about 3 minutes or until pureed. Using the back of a wooden spoon, force the puree through a non-reactive strainer set over a medium bowl.

5. Carefully place each pear upright in the center of a dessert plate. Discard the poaching liquid. Spoon the puree over and around the base of each pear, sprinkle the pears with

the chive petals, and serve at once. If desired, accompany with dessert cheese and sweet crackers.

Curried Shallot Shortbread

Makes 3 dozen

(Can be made up to 2 days ahead.)

Spirited in flavor, these pale yellow shortbread cookies are savory, with little morsels of shallots and spice, yet the shallots add enough sweetness to transform them into a dessert item. Use them to offset a docile dessert such as a mild cheese or fruit. They are a terrific accompaniment to pineapple or berry sorbet. My well-traveled friend Judith suggests serving them with mango ice cream, which can be found in some Indian grocery stores. (The cayenne is optional. Use it if you want to serve the cookies as a savory snack—they are wonderful with a glass of sherry at the end of the day—with a salad or entree, or as hors d'oeuvres with a tart goat cheese or English cheddar. Omit the cayenne if the shortbread is to be served as a dessert.)

Butter, not margarine, is a must for this recipe, because margarine lends a "fishy" flavor, and not as much depth as butter.

3 1/4 cups unbleached all-purpose white flour, plus more to dust

1/3 cup sugar

1 1/2 teaspoons curry powder

1   teaspoon salt

1 1/2 cups (3 sticks) unsalted butter, cut into small dice and chilled, plus more to grease baking sheets

6   ounces shallots, very thinly sliced (for a quick method of peeling see directions on page 48)

1/4 cup honey

1/2 teaspoon cayenne (ground red pepper, optional)

1. Sift together the flour, sugar, curry powder, and salt in a large bowl. Using a pastry blender or fork, cut the cold butter into the flour mixture until it resembles coarse crumbs. Stir in the shallots, honey, and cayenne (if desired) until blended and a soft dough forms. Press the dough into a ball, wrap it in waxed paper, and freeze for 20 minutes.

2. Preheat the oven to 350°F. Lightly butter 2 baking sheets.

3. Cut the dough into 9 equal portions, break off 4 walnut-size pieces from each portion, then roll each piece between well-floured palms to form 36 evenly sized balls. Using the palm of your hand, press each ball flat, until 2 inches in diameter, and place $1/2$ inch apart onto the prepared baking sheets.

4. Bake in the middle third of the oven for 12 to 15 minutes or until lightly golden around the edges. (*Note:* If you desire a crisper cookie, bake for 15 to 18 minutes or until light golden brown all over.)

5. Using a spatula, carefully transfer the fragile shortbread cookies to a wire rack to cool. Serve at room temperature. Store layers between sheets of waxed paper in an airtight container, such as a tin, in a cool, dry place for up to 2 days. Do not refrigerate.

Onion-Cassis Sorbet

Serves 8

This sorbet can be served as a dessert or as an *intermezzo*—a refreshing palate cleanser served between courses. It is equally effective alongside a luncheon of cold meats. Serve in small amounts, for this sorbet is meant to be savored. I like to use a melon baller, placing the scoops in Champagne cups, then garnishing them with chives, so that guests are anticipating the novel taste.

Though unexpected, the flavors of onion, grape, and *cassis* are meant for each other. The onion adds spark, while the grape juice lends a beautiful reddish-purple color. I use an all-natural purple grape juice, such as Welch's, made with Concord grapes. You can substitute white grape juice for a golden-colored sorbet.

1 cup sugar

3/4 cup water

2 cups purple or white grape juice

2 cups finely chopped sweet mild onion, such as Walla Walla, California Sweet Imperial, Vidalia, Texas 1015 SuperSweet, or Maui

1/2 cup fresh lemon juice (from 2 to 3 medium lemons)

3 tablespoons *crème de cassis* (black currant liqueur)

Finely chopped fresh chives, to garnish

1. Combine the sugar, water, grape juice, onion, lemon juice, and liqueur in the container of a blender. Cover and blend on medium speed about 3 minutes or until pureed. Force the puree through a fine sieve into an 8-inch-square baking dish, discarding any solids. Using a fork, pop any air bubbles in the mixture.

2. Cover the dish tightly with plastic wrap and freeze for 2 hours or until ice crystals form 1 inch around the edge of the mixture. Spoon into the blender container, cover, and blend on high speed about 15 seconds or until smooth. Return the mixture to the baking dish, cover tightly, and return to the freezer. Freeze for 10 hours or overnight, until the mixture is firm. Scoop into Champagne cups, garnish with chives, and serve.

Walnut-Shallot Biscotti

Makes about 3 dozen

Biscotti—twice-baked Italian cookies—are meant to be dipped, their crisp, dry texture acting like a sponge, absorbing the liquid of choice. For this recipe, I recommend dipping walnut-shallot *biscotti* into red wine or sherry, for a delightful treat after a meal, but before the dessert or coffee. The nutty overtones of the shallots support the flavor of the walnuts, creating a balance of sophisticated and complex flavors.

Canola oil, to grease baking sheet

$2\frac{1}{4}$ cups unbleached all-purpose white flour

1 teaspoon double-acting baking powder

$\frac{1}{4}$ teaspoon salt

$\frac{3}{4}$ cup sugar

2 large eggs

$\frac{1}{8}$ cup finely chopped shallots macerated in $\frac{1}{4}$ cup dry red wine for 10 minutes and drained, reserving 1 tablespoon of the macerating liquid

6 ounces ($1\frac{1}{2}$ cups) walnuts, toasted on a baking sheet in a 350°F oven for 7 minutes and coarsely chopped

1 teaspoon freshly ground black pepper

1. Preheat the oven to 350°F. Lightly oil a baking sheet and cover with parchment paper.

2. Sift together the flour, baking powder, and salt in a medium bowl. In a large bowl whisk together the sugar and eggs until well blended. Stir in the drained macerated shallots, the 1 tablespoon reserved macerating liquid, walnuts, and pepper, until well blended. Sift the flour mixture over the egg mixture, and using a rubber spatula fold until just combined and there is no trace of flour. (*Note:* The dough may at first appear sticky, but do not add more flour or the *biscotti* will be heavy and dense.)

3. Divide the dough in half and transfer each to the prepared baking sheet. Using floured hands, pinch and stretch each portion of dough into an evenly formed 13- by 2-inch log, placing them about 3 inches apart on the baking sheet. Pat each log to smooth the surface.

4. Bake in the middle third of the oven for 35 minutes, turning the baking sheet once after the first 15 minutes, or until the loaves are golden and just beginning to crack on top. (*Note:* The loaves will flatten and spread as they bake.)

5. Remove the baking sheet from the oven, and let the loaves cool on the sheet for 10 minutes.

6. Reduce the oven temperature to 325°F. Using a serrated knife, cut each loaf diagonally into ¾-inch-thick slices. Lay the slices, cut side up, about ½ inch apart on the baking sheet and return them to the oven. Bake in the middle third of the oven for 15 minutes, turning each cookie over after the first 7 minutes, or until the surface becomes crisp. Transfer the *biscotti* to a wire rack and cool completely. (*Note:* As the *biscotti* cool to room temperature, they will become crisp throughout.) Store in an airtight tin at room temperature up to 3 days.

Pear-Apple Pastry with Wilted Leeks

Makes one 9-inch pie, serves 6 to 8

(Dough can be made up to 2 days ahead.)

In this recipe, the edges of the dough are folded over the filling to form a pie that is slightly open-faced: the filling is exposed in the center. This unusual form was inspired by the *Peach Pouch Pie with Berries* in an article by Peggy Cullen in the August 1994 issue of *Food & Wine* magazine. The leeks complement the pears, enhancing their flavor, while the apples provide a background flavor note, their natural pectin acting as a thickening agent for the filling. Serve each wedge of this peasant-style pie alongside a slice of Italian Fontina cheese from Val d'Aosta, a medium-sharp cheddar like English Farmhouse, or a tangy goat cheese like Bûcheron for a savory dessert.

Crust

2 cups unbleached all-purpose flour, plus more to dust

1/2 cup sugar

1/2 cup (1 stick) unsalted butter, cut into small dice and chilled

Freshly grated lemon zest, from 1 medium lemon

1 large egg

1 large egg yolk lightly whisked with 2 tablespoons ice water, plus 1 tablespoon more water, if needed

Filling

2 1/2 cups water

1/4 cup fresh lemon juice

1 1/4 pounds Cortland or Rome apples

2 pounds ripe Red Bartlett or Comice pears

1/2 cup sugar

2 tablespoons French *poire william* (pear brandy)

1/2 cup well washed, very thinly sliced leeks (white part only)

Italian Fontina cheese from Val d'Aosta, English Farmhouse cheddar cheese, or Bûcheron, at room temperature, to serve

1. To prepare the crust: Sift together the flour and sugar in a medium bowl. Using a pastry blender or fork, cut in the chilled butter until the mixture resembles coarse crumbs. Stir in the lemon zest, egg, and egg yolk with water until well blended, and the mixture just holds together in large clumps. Make sure there are no streaks of egg yolk. If needed to form a soft dough, stir in an additional table-spoon of ice water. Gather together dough clumps and form into a flat disk. Wrap tightly with waxed paper and refrigerate for 1 hour. (Dough can be made up to 2 days ahead.)

2. To make the filling: Stir together 1¹/₄ cups water and half of the lemon juice in a medium bowl until well combined. Peel and core the apples and cut them into 1-inch irregular chunks, stirring them into the water/lemon juice mixture to prevent discoloration while cutting. Repeat the process with the pears.

3. Transfer the apple-pear mixture with the liquid and remaining lemon juice and 1¹/₄ more cups of water to a heavy, nonreactive 4¹/₂- to 5-quart saucepan and place over high heat. Stir in the sugar, *poire william,* and leeks until well combined and bring to a boil. Reduce the heat to medium-low and simmer, partially covered, stirring occasionally for 20 to 30 minutes until the apples are just tender—some may begin to fall apart, but most remain in chunks. Using a slotted spoon, measure out 3 cups of the filling for the pie (leaving behind excess juice) and let cool completely, saving any remaining filling and the juice for another use.

4. On a lightly floured work surface, roll out the chilled dough into a 14-inch round. Line a 9-inch pie plate with the dough, and gently press the dough against the bottom and sides of the pan without stretching it. Using a pastry wheel, trim the crust to leave a 2-inch overhang. Refrigerate for 30 minutes.

5. Preheat the oven to 450°F.

6. Using a slotted spoon, ladle the filling into the pie shell and distribute it evenly. Fold the dough overhang toward the center, pleating as needed. Cover only the outer area of the filling and leave a 5-inch opening of exposed filling in the center of the pie.

7. Place a sheet of aluminum foil on the middle of the oven rack (to catch any drips) and bake the pie in the middle third of the oven for 25 to 35 minutes, or until the crust is golden. Let the pie cool slightly in its pan on a wire rack for 10 minutes. Serve warm alongside the cheese.

Pine Nut–Scallion Brittle

Makes about 1½ pounds

Many nations have candies that are made with what are considered savory or rather, unsweet ingredients. For example, Hawaii candies seaweed; China, ginger root; and Mexico, squash and its seeds. So it seemed natural to me to pair pine nuts (*pignoli*) and scallions in a crunchy candy brittle. Pine nuts are the edible seeds of pine trees. They are slightly soft and have a satiny patina, and a captivating hint of resin flavor. The scallions add a slight, enticing peppery bite and faint oniony background to the flavorful nuts.

Make sure you have all your ingredients prepared and your equipment on hand before beginning this recipe. The process of making candy happens quickly, and you won't have time in between the different cooking stages to chop or gather. Also, a candy thermometer needs to be tested before its initial use and occasionally thereafter for accurate recipe results. To do this, place the thermometer in a saucepan with enough cold water to cover the bulb. Bring to a boil; continue boiling for 2 minutes. Read the temperature at eye level and note the temperature at which the water boils; it should read 212°F at or near sea level. If it reads a degree or two above or below 212°F, adjust the cooking temperatures in this recipe accordingly by adding or subtracting the number of degrees of variance you have from 212°F. One last tip: Do not try to make brittle in humid weather; it will not harden completely and will be sticky, as it draws moisture from the air.

For easy clean-up, soak the pan used to make the brittle in very hot water to help dissolve and remove the candy.

Butter, to grease pan

¼ cup heavy cream, at room temperature

¼ cup light corn syrup (do not use dark)

¼ cup water

1 cup sugar

½ cup (1 stick) unsalted butter

¼ teaspoon salt

$^1/_2$ teaspoon baking soda

$^1/_2$ teaspoon vanilla extract

$^1/_4$ cup *very* thinly sliced scallions, including greens, dried thoroughly between paper towels (*Note:* It is important to cut the scallions as thinly as possible and to remove as much water as possible)

8 ounces (1$^3/_4$ cups) pine nuts (*pignoli*)

1. Liberally butter a 15- by 10-inch jelly-roll pan and set aside. Combine the cream, corn syrup, water, and sugar in a heavy 4-quart saucepan and stir together until well blended. Place the saucepan over medium-high heat and stir until the mixture comes to a boil. If you see sugar crystals on the inside of the saucepan, use a wet pastry brush to wash down the sides.

2. Continue cooking the syrup until it reaches 295°F on a candy thermometer. (*Note:* If necessary, tilt the pan to allow the thermometer to reach the liquid, to make sure you get an accurate reading.) Stir in the butter (which will lower the temperature) and cook the syrup until, when tested by dropping a small amount of syrup into a cup of very cold water, the syrup separates into threads that are hard but not brittle (280°F).

3. Remove the saucepan from the heat, and wearing flameproof oven mitts to avoid sugar or steam burns immediately stir in the salt, baking soda, vanilla, scallions, and pine nuts. Stir very briefly, just until the nuts are coated. Pour onto the prepared jelly-roll pan.

4. Working quickly, using the back of a wooden spoon, press the brittle into a smooth, even layer. Let stand at room temperature until cooled completely and hard, about 1 hour.

5. Break the brittle into pieces and serve. Store in layers between sheets of waxed paper in an airtight container, such as a tin, and keep in a cool, dry place for up to 3 days. Do not refrigerate.

White Chocolate "Pearl" Onions

Makes 3½ dozen

These surprisingly shaped candies have the pearl color and shape of delicate white onions and make a nice dessert to serve in autumn on account of their harvest theme. Serve in a cloth napkin-lined, plastic-mesh pearl onion basket for added effect.

You make these with white chocolate plastic, or "plastique," a pliable, edible chocolate mixture that can be formed into many shapes or structures. It is also delicious. The texture of these rich candies is similar to a white chocolate version of Tootsie Rolls, only mine are each filled with a hidden hazelnut.

16 ounces white chocolate, coarsely chopped

½ cup light corn syrup (do not use dark)

Confectioners' sugar, to dust

42 shelled whole hazelnuts, skins removed (how-to procedure follows)

1. In the top of a double boiler set over hot water just below simmering, melt the chocolate. The chocolate should melt very gently; if it becomes too hot it will be flecked with light spots. Stir the chocolate frequently for 3 to 4 minutes or just until smooth. (*Note:* Do not let any water drop into the chocolate. If it does, start over.)

2. Remove the top pan from the bottom pan and immediately transfer the chocolate to a mixing bowl. Let stand for 5 to 10 minutes or until the chocolate cools to room temperature, but does not set. In a slow, steady stream, pour in and beat the corn syrup at low speed for 30 seconds or until the mixture thickens, begins to lose its shine, and forms a soft, dough-like mixture, scraping down the sides of the bowl as needed. Form into a ball, wrap tightly in a double layer of

plastic wrap, place in a plastic bag, and let sit at room temperature overnight.

3. The next day, unwrap the chocolate and bring to room temperature so that it becomes soft enough to work with. Place on a work surface lightly dusted with confectioners' sugar and knead until soft and smooth. (*Note:* If it is humid, the chocolate might be too soft and sticky to work with; if so, knead more confectioners' sugar into it.)

4. To form the candy, cut into 42 evenly sized pieces. Press a hazelnut, pointed end first, into the center of each piece. Dust your hands lightly with confectioners' sugar, then roll each piece into a ball $3/4$ inch in diameter, so that the hazelnut is completely covered.

5. One by one, pinch the ends of each ball between your thumb and index finger to create a tapered end, and then bend the tapered end slightly to the right, so that the candy resembles a pearl onion. Repeat with the remaining candy balls.

6. Serve at room temperature. Store in layers between sheets of waxed paper in an airtight container, such as a tin, at room temperature. Do not refrigerate.

TO REMOVE HAZELNUT SKINS

Arrange the hazelnuts in a single layer on a baking sheet. Bake in a preheated 350°F oven, stirring occasionally for 10 to 15 minutes. (*Note:* They should only be toasted a light golden brown. Do not let them burn.)

Working quickly, slide the hot nuts from the baking sheet onto a dish towel, and wrap them tightly in the towel. Let steam about 1 minute. Rub the hazelnuts in the towel until the skins flake off. (*Note:* Not all the skins will come off.) Let cool completely before using.

Resources

The following list includes some select mail-order sources for onions, garlic, leeks, chives, and other alliums. For your convenience, many suppliers now accept phone and fax orders, too.

ONION ASSOCIATIONS AND COMMITTEES

California Imperial Sweet Onion Commission
P.O. Box 3575
El Centro, CA 92244
(619) 353-1900

Call for mail-order sources that sell California Sweet Imperial onions.

Fresh Garlic Association
Caryl Saunders Associates
P.O. Box 2410
Sausalito, CA 94966
(415) 383-5057

Call for mail-order sources that sell garlic and to secure answers to garlic-related questions.

Fresno County Sweet Onion Committee
1720 South Maple Avenue
Fresno, CA 93702
(209) 456-7285

Call for mail-order sources that sell Fresno Sweets.

Maui Farmers Cooperative Exchange
970-B Lower Main Street
Wailuku, Maui, HI 96793
(808) 242-9767

Call for mail-order sources that sell Maui onions.

National Onion Association
One Greeley National Plaza
Suite 510
Greeley, CO 80631
(303) 353-5895

Direct any onion-related questions to this association.

South Texas Onion Committee
P.O. Box 2587
McAllen, TX 78502
(210) 686-9538

Call for mail-order sources that sell Texas 1015 SuperSweet onions.

Vidalia Onion Committee
P.O. Box 1609
Vidalia, GA 30474
(912) 537-1918

Call for mail-order sources that
sell Vidalia onions.

**Walla Walla Sweet Onion
Commission**
P.O. Box 644
Walla Walla, WA 99362
(509) 525-0850

Call for mail-order sources that
sell Walla Walla Sweet onions.

READY-TO-EAT ALLIUMS

Arbini Farms
Route 1, Box 347
Walla Walla, WA 99362
(509) 525-5599

Walla Walla Sweet onions; free
price list; mail order

Aux Delices des Bois
4 Leonard Street
New York, NY 10013
(212) 334-1230
1-800-666-1232

Wild mushrooms and other
hard-to-find wild edibles such as
ramps; free price list; mail order

Bland Farms
P.O. Box 506
Glennville, GA 30427-0506
1-800-843-2542

Vidalia onions and Baby Vidalias;
free catalog; mail order

Frank Lewis Co.
100 North Tower Road
Alamo, TX 78516
(210) 787-9971
1-800-477-4773

Fresno Sweets; free price list;
mail order

**Frieda's Finest Produce
Specialties, Inc.**
P.O. Box 58488
Los Angeles, CA 90058
(213) 627-2981

Cipolline; call for product
information.

G & R Farms of Georgia, Inc.
Route 3, Box 35A
Glennville, GA 30427
(912) 654-1534

Vidalia onions; free price list;
mail order

Garlic World
4800 Monterey Highway
Gilroy, CA 95020
(408) 847-2251
1-800-537-6122

Various varieties of fresh garlic;
free catalog; mail order

H. F. Allen Company
P.O. Box 180
Conaway Road
Vidalia, GA 30474
1-800-673-6338

Vidalia onions; free price list;
mail order

Humphrey's Gift Fruit
P.O. Box 1436
Los Fresnos, TX 78566
1-800-828-4458

Texas 1015 SuperSweet onions;
free price list; mail order

Jungle King of California, Inc.
7929 East Manning Avenue
Fowler, CA 93625
(209) 834-1249

Italian sweet red onions; free
price list; mail order

Lone Star Farms
P.O. Box 685
Mercedes, TX 78570
1-800-552-1015

Texas 1015 SuperSweet onions;
free price list; mail order

Mountain Meadow Farm
826 Ulrich Road
Prospect, OR 97536
(503) 560-3350

Various varieties of organically
grown fresh garlic; free brochure;
mail order

Nelson Farms
Route #2
Box 297
Anthony, NM 88021
(505) 882-2258

Nu-Mex Sweet onions; free
price list; mail order

Ontario Produce Company, Inc.
P.O. Box 880
Ontario, OR 97914
1-800-848-7799

Spanish Sweet onions; free price
list; mail order

Robison Ranch
P.O. Box 1018
Walla Walla, WA 99362
(509) 525-8807

Shallots; free catalog; mail order

The Allium Connection
1339 Swainwood Drive
Glenview, IL 60025
(708) 729-4823

Shallots; phone orders; mail order

Valley Gin and Onion Shed
P.O. Box 288
Columbus, NM 88029
(505) 531-2219

Carzalia onions; free price list;
mail order

PLANTS, SEEDS, AND SEEDLINGS

Filaree Farm
Route #1
Box 162
Okanogan, WA 98840
(509) 422-6940

Over 200 organically grown
strains of garlic for home-grow-
ing; also available *Growing Great
Garlic,* an extremely informative
book; free catalog; mail order

Kalmia Farm
P.O. Box 3881
Charlottesville, VA 22903

Multiplier onions, potato onions, Egyptian top onions, exotic shallot varieties, and some garlic varieties; write for catalog.

Native Seeds/Search
2509 North Campbell Avenue
Room #325
Tucson, AZ 85719
(602) 327-9123

Unusual heirloom and native onion and garlic varieties; free catalog; mail order

Nichols Garden Nursery
1190 North Pacific Highway
Albany, OR 97321
(503) 928-9280

Chives, Oriental garlic chives, and other alliums; free catalog; mail order

Seeds Blüm
Idaho City Stage
Boise, ID 83706
(208) 342-0858

A wide variety of heirloom seeds, among them unusual alliums; send $3 for catalog; mail order

Seed Savers Exchange
R.R. 3, Box 239
Decorah, IA 52101

Members include farmers and serious gardeners dedicated to saving and trading seeds of heirloom vegetables and plants to protect and maintain unusual varieties for future generations. Contact by mail for membership information.

Shepherd's Garden Seeds
30 Irene Street
Torrington, CT 06790
CT (203) 482-3638
CA (408) 335-6910

Good selection of shallots, onion plants and seeds, garlic, and scallions, including Japanese Red Beard scallions; send $1.00 for catalog; mail order

Southern Exposure Seed Exchange
P.O. Box 170
Earlysville, VA 22936
(804) 973-4703

Potato onions, shallots, and Egyptian top onions; send $2.00 for catalog; mail order

Sunrise Enterprises
P.O. Box 330058
West Hartford, CT 06133
(203) 666-8071

Alliums, including Japanese bunching onions, and Chinese leek flowers; send $2.00 for catalog; mail order

The Cook's Garden
P.O. Box 535
Londonderry, VT 05148
(802) 824-3400

Wide variety of alliums, including Florence long red onions, and a good selection of leeks and boiling onions; free catalog; mail order

McClure & Zimmerman
P.O. Box 368
Friesland, WI 53935
(414) 326-4220

Free catalog; mail order

Smith and Hawken
25 Corte Madera Avenue
Mill Valley, CA 94941
(415) 383-2000

Free catalog; mail order

White Flower Farm
Litchfield, CT 06759
(203) 496-9600

Send $5.00 for catalog; mail
order

Food History News
Isleboro, ME 04848
(207) 734-8140

Call for subscription information
to this newsletter.

Greenmarket Farmers' Market
130 East 16th Street
New York, NY 10003
(212) 477-3220

When in New York City call for a
tour of this wonderful market.

The Historical Gardener
1910 North 35th Place
Mt. Vernon, WA 98273
(206) 424-3154

Write or call for subscription
information to this newsletter.

ONION FESTIVITIES

Here are some of the many allium-related festivals from which to choose:

Bern Switzerland Onion Festival
Bern, Switzerland
For information: Call the Swiss National Tourist Office at (212) 757-5944.

Chez Panisse Garlic Festival
Berkeley, California
For information: Call Chez Panisse at (415) 548-5525.

Cosby Ramp Festival
Newport, Tennessee
For information: Call the Nashville Department of Tourist Development at (615) 741-2159.

Feast of the Ramson
Richwood, West Virginia
For information: Call the West Virginia Chamber of Commerce at (304) 846-6790.

Garlic Fest
Covington, Kentucky
For information: Call the Northern Kentucky Convention and Visitors Bureau at (606) 261-4677.

Gilroy Garlic Festival
Gilroy, California
For information: Call the Gilroy Garlic Festival Association at (408) 842-1625.

Hudson Valley Garlic Festival
Saugerties, New York
For information: Call Shale Hill Farm and Herb Gardens at (914) 246-6982.

Maui Onion Festival
Maui, Hawaii
For information: Call Kaanapali Beach Resort at (808) 661-4567.

Vacaville Onion Festival
Vacaville, California
For information: Call Lou Soucie, Publicist for Vacaville Onion Festival at (415) 573-9250.

Vidalia Sweet Onion Festival
Vidalia, Georgia
For information: Call the Vidalia Tourism Council Office at (912) 538-8687.

A Select Bibliography

Over the course of writing this book, I researched scores of articles and books on onions and related topics. What follows is an abbreviated list of that fascinating reading.

Aresty, Esther B. *The Delectable Past.* New York: Simon and Schuster, Inc., 1964.

Bianchini, Francesco, and Francesco Corbetta. *The Complete Book of Fruit and Vegetables.* New York: Crown Publishers, Inc., 1975.

Crawford, Stanley. *A Garlic Testament.* New York: HarperCollins Publishers, 1992.

Creasy, Rosalind. *Cooking from the Garden.* San Francisco: Sierra Club Books, 1988.

Engeland, Ron L. *Growing Great Garlic.* Okanogan, Washington: Filaree Productions, 1992.

Ferrary, Jeannette, and Louise Fiszer. *Sweet Onions & Sour Cherries.* New York: Simon and Schuster, Inc., 1992.

Gibbons, Euell. *Stalking the Wild Asparagus.* New York: David McKay Company, Inc., 1962.

Root, Waverley. *Food.* New York: Simon and Schuster, Inc., 1980.

Rossant, Colette, and Marianne Melendez. *Vegetables.* New York: The Penguin Group, 1991.

Singer, Marilyn. *The Fanatic's Ecstatic Aromatic Guide to Onions, Garlic, Shallots and Leeks.* Englewood Cliffs, New Jersey: Prentice-Hall, Inc., 1981.

Sokolov, Raymond. *Why We Eat What We Eat.* New York: Simon and Schuster, Inc., 1991.

Stone, Sally, and Martin Stone. *The Essential Root Vegetable Cookbook.* New York: Clarkson Potter, 1991.

Tannahill, Reay. *Food in History.* New York: Stein and Day Publishers, 1973.

Index

About the Author

As a professional cook and food stylist with degrees in both photography and design and the culinary arts, Mara Reid Rogers has a food industry background both varied and extensive. Former assistant food and entertaining editor at *House Beautiful Magazine,* she lives in Atlanta, Georgia, where she works as a freelance food consultant. She is the author of *Contemporary One-Dish Meals* (Lake Isle Press, Inc., 1991), *Creative Garnishing* (Running Press, Inc., 1991), *The International Spud* (Little, Brown & Co., 1992), and *The Instant Ethnic Cook* (Lake Isle Press, Inc., 1993).